Chetna Makan

CLASSIC
INDIAN
RECIPES

Chetna Makan

CLASSIC INDIAN RECIPES

75 signature dishes

hamlyn

First published in Great Britain in 2025
by Hamlyn, an imprint of
Octopus Publishing Group Ltd
Carmelite House
50 Victoria Embankment
London EC4Y 0DZ
www.octopusbooks.co.uk

An Hachette UK Company
www.hachette.co.uk

The authorised representative in the EEA is Hachette Ireland,
8 Castlecourt Centre, Castleknock Road,
Castleknock, Dublin 15, D15 YF6A, Ireland

Some of this material previously appeared in *Chetna's 30 Minute Indian*, *Chai, Chaat & Chutney*, *Chetna's Indian Feasts*, *Chetna's Healthy Indian* and *Chetna's Healthy Indian Vegetarian*.

ISBN 978-0-600-63888-9

A CIP catalogue record for this book is available from the British Library

Printed and bound in China

10 9 8 7 6 5 4 3 2 1

Publisher: Lucy Pessell
Designer: Isobel Platt
Photographer: Nassima Rothacker
Editor: Feyi Oyesanya
Assistant Editor: Samina Rahman
Production Manager: Allison Gonsalves

Both metric and imperial measurements are given for the recipes.
Use one set of measures only, not a mixture of both.

Ovens should be preheated to the specified temperature. If using a fan-assisted oven, follow the manufacturer's instructions for adjusting the time and temperature. Grills should also be preheated.

This books includes dishes made with nuts and nut derivatives. It is advisable for those with known allergic reactions to nuts and nut derivatives and those who may be potentially vulnerable to these allergies, such as pregnant and nursing mothers, invalids, the elderly, babies and children, to avoid dishes made with nuts and nut oils. It is also prudent to check the labels of preprepared ingredients for the possible inclusion of nut derivatives.

The Department of Health advises that eggs should not be consumed raw. This book contains some dishes made with raw or lightly cooked eggs. It is prudent for more vulnerable people such as pregnant and nursing mothers, invalids, the elderly, babies and young children to avoid uncooked or lightly cooked dishes made with eggs.

Meat and poultry should be cooked thoroughly. To test if poultry is cooked, pierce the flesh through the thickest part with a skewer or fork – the juices should run clear, never pink or red.

CONTENTS

INTRODUCTION

To try and summarize Indian cuisine is not an easy task. India is a large, diverse country and the food varies from region to region. Northern India, for example, is known as India's bread basket, and its dishes are often accompanied by roti or paratha. In South India, coconut trees are abundant, so coconut is often a key ingredient here. Some regions, such as the state of Gujarat, are predominantly vegetarian due to religious reasons, while coastal India is known for its unique seafood dishes. From the mouthwatering chaat of Jabalpur (the small town in central India where I grew up) to the dosa and sambhar of South India, India's food culture is both delicious and diverse.

And India's food culture doesn't stop in India – look no further than the now-traditional British Friday night curry, a concept that was totally new to me when I moved to the UK many years ago but one that I have whole-heartedly embraced.

A common thread in Indian cuisine is the emphasis on delicious, fresh ingredients. Growing up, my mum would buy fresh veg from the street vendor who came calling to our road every morning and choose her dishes for the day based on what he was selling. If she bought enough vegetables, he would throw in some green chillies and a lime for free, so you can imagine how fresh our meals were.

Staple ingredients include rice, wholewheat flour and a wide variety of lentils and pulses, and of course you'll find these in many of the recipes throughout this book. Popular spices include cardamom, cumin, turmeric, ginger, coriander and the favoured spice mix garam masala.

Narrowing down 75 recipes was no mean feat, but I have selected recipes that reflect various key elements of Indian cuisine, from street food staples and sweet treats to delectable dals and flavourful curries. Whether you are entertaining friends and family or rustling up a simple midweek meal, I hope you will find plenty to enjoy in this book.

The Indian menu

Chaat (sour and spicy street food snacks): Street food is a huge and important part of India's food culture. Most street food is freshly prepared to order, served very quickly and, best of all, extremely cheap. My family's street food favourites were the chaat – bhel puri, pani puri and papdi chaat. The stall that made the best chaat in Jabalpur still exists! The next generation of stallholders gradually learned the tricks of the trade, so whenever I visit my parents, I make sure to go there and enjoy some more of what I consider to be the best chaat I've ever tasted.

Vegetarian dishes: I grew up in India, so vegetarianism is not new to me. My dad is vegetarian and so are many of my friends and relatives. Many of my go-to recipes are vegetarian and contain lots of fresh, seasonal vegetables, which are not only low in fat but packed full of nutrients and fibre, which we all know are good for you.

Meat and fish: Fish is a great source of protein and contains lots of minerals, including calcium and much more, making it a very healthy choice. Similarly, chicken is not just delicious, but brilliant for all its protein, minerals and vitamins. I've included a variety of flavour-packed yet super-simple curries.

Dals: I tend to cook a lot with lentils – a great source of protein, fibre, vitamins and much more. They are easy to store and cook, so are brilliant for midweek meals. But the best part, as far as I'm concerned, is the huge variety of lentils there is to choose from. Each type has a unique texture and flavour; if I specify a type of lentil in a recipe and you choose another one, the result will not be as intended. Don't worry – it can still taste great, but factors such as the flavour, texture and cooking time will need to change. So please do try to use the specified lentils in each recipe to get the best results.

Rice and breads: Of course, a curry needs to be enjoyed with rice or roti. These are a key part of any Indian meal. The rice recipes here are varied and many work perfectly as meals on their own, such as Peanut, Coriander and Lemon Rice or Aubergine and Potato Rice. The flatbreads are also brilliant and can be served with any of the curries in this book.

Chutneys and sides: All my friends know how much I love chutney and pickles! I believe adding a dollop of good chutney to your meal can make it extraordinary. The ingredients used in them are super-healthy too. Turn a simple flatbread into a feast of a snack with some pickle, make your lentils a little more special with a chutney or elevate your curry with a raita.

Sweet things: If you're someone who needs to finish meals with a little something sweet, that's exactly what you'll find here. Desserts are an important part of Indian cuisine, irresistibly sweet and rich with flavour. The desserts and treats here are mostly bite-size – ideal for enjoying in moderation. Whether it's a delicious Almond Halwa or a refreshing glass of Mango Lassi, these sweet treats are the perfect finishing touch for any meal.

CHAAT

Dahi Puri

SERVES 4
1 medium potato,
  peeled, boiled and
  cooled
50 ml (2 fl oz) water
200 ml (7 fl oz) natural
  yogurt
24 puris (pani puri)
tamarind jaggery
  chutney, to taste
coriander yogurt
  chutney, to taste
¼ teaspoon salt
¼ teaspoon chilli
  powder
¼ teaspoon chaat
  masala
nylon sev (gram flour
  noodles), to taste

This dahi puri is a version of the popular snack pani puri, but instead of spicy water, the puri is filled with yogurt before being topped with a medley of flavours. Puris are readily available in Asian shops by the name of pani puri, as is 'nylon' sev, which is just a quirky name for superfine sev, a crunchy snack made with gram (besan/chickpea) flour. You can prepare all the elements beforehand, but put the dish together just before serving so that it retains its satisfying crispiness.

1 Break up the boiled potato roughly by hand.

2 Whisk the measured water and yogurt in a bowl until the mixture is smooth.

3 When you are ready to serve, place the puris on a dish and, using your thumb, gently break the top of each one to make a small opening. Load up each puri with a little of the potato, then add a good tablespoon or more of the yogurt on top. Now drizzle over some of the tamarind and coriander chutneys. Sprinkle the salt, chilli powder and chaat masala on top, then scatter the sev over the puris to finish. Serve immediately.

Crispy Paneer Cubes

SERVES 2

2 tablespoons gram
  flour (besan)
70 ml (2½ fl oz)
  natural yogurt
¼ teaspoon salt
1 teaspoon kashmiri
  chilli powder
1 teaspoon kasuri
  methi (dried
  fenugreek leaves)
½ teaspoon amchur
  (mango powder)
½ teaspoon garam
  masala
½ teaspoon ground
  cumin
200 g (7 oz) paneer,
  cut into 2.5 cm
  (1 inch) cubes
sunflower oil, for
  shallow-frying

Snack, light meal, side or starter – I don't know how to categorize this dish. In India, you would serve it as a snack with some chai or even as a starter, however heavy the meal to follow (there is always room for fried paneer). The spiced yogurt is a great marinade, with the addition of gram flour ensuring that it sticks to the paneer. Toasting the flour is important, as it eliminates the raw taste, resulting in a delicious and crisp paneer. Serve with some coriander chutney.

1 Heat a frying pan, add the flour and toast over a low heat for about 2 minutes until it starts to change colour, stirring constantly.

2 Put the toasted flour into a bowl with the yogurt, salt and spices and mix together well. Add the paneer cubes and gently turn in the marinade until well coated.

3 Heat enough oil for shallow-frying in a frying pan. Carefully add the paneer to the hot oil and cook over a medium–high heat for 1–2 minutes, turning halfway through, until golden and crispy. Serve warm.

Cheesy Potato Balls

MAKES 8

2 potatoes, peeled and cut into 1 cm (½ inch) pieces
1 tablespoon sunflower oil, plus extra for deep-frying
1 green chilli, finely chopped
10 fresh curry leaves, finely chopped
½ teaspoon black mustard seeds
½ teaspoon salt
½ teaspoon chilli powder
½ teaspoon ground turmeric
1 tablespoon water
30 g (1 oz) Cheddar cheese, cut into small cubes

FOR THE BATTER

100 g (3½ oz) gram flour (besan)
½ teaspoon salt
½ teaspoon chilli powder
½ teaspoon ground turmeric
about 120 ml (4 fl oz) water

This widely loved snack in India, which is famed in Mumbai as batata vada, is customarily sold in a soft bun with a garlic and chilli chutney. Its popularity has spread and it's now available in many Indian restaurants worldwide. Where I come from, these delicious potato balls are called alu banda and are sold in small shops and street stalls in the mornings for breakfast with chai. So why not serve this with some coriander chutney and piping hot masala chai?

1   Put the potato pieces in a pan and cover with water. Bring to the boil and cook for 5 minutes until tender. Drain and set aside.

2   Heat the 1 tablespoon of oil in a pan and add the green chilli, curry leaves and mustard seeds. Once they start to sizzle, stir in the salt and ground spices and cook over a low heat for a few seconds. Add the measured water and the cooked potatoes and mix well, then leave to cool while you make the batter.

3   Mix together all the batter ingredients except the water in a bowl. Then gradually whisk in enough of the water to make a smooth batter with a coating consistency.

4   Divide the potato mixture into 8 portions and form each into a ball about the size of a lime. Push a cube of cheese into the centre of each potato ball and mould the potato mixture back around it to seal it in.

5   Heat enough oil for deep-frying in a deep-fat fryer or deep, heavy-based pan (ensuring the pan is no more than one-third full) to 180°C (350°F). Line a plate with kitchen paper. Dip one potato ball at a time into the batter and then carefully add to the hot oil. Deep-fry, in small batches, for a minute on each side until golden. Transfer to the paper-lined plate to absorb the excess oil while you fry the remaining balls. Serve warm.

Bhakarwadi

MAKES 60
sunflower oil, for
deep-frying

FOR THE PASTRY
150 g (5½ oz) plain
flour
50 g (1¾ oz) gram flour
(besan)
¼ teaspoon salt
¼ teaspoon ground
turmeric
about 100 ml
(3½ fl oz) water

FOR THE FILLING
25 g (1 oz) sesame seeds
25 g (1 oz) white
poppy seeds
25 g (1 oz) desiccated
coconut
1 teaspoon fennel
seeds
1 teaspoon sunflower
oil
1 teaspoon finely
chopped ginger
1 tablespoon gram
flour (besan)
½ teaspoon salt
½ teaspoon chilli
powder
1½ teaspoon
granulated sugar
1 teaspoon ground
coriander
1 teaspoon ground
cumin

These tiny sweet-savoury snacks are found at most of the tea stalls in Mumbai. The pastry is filled with beautiful spices and fried to give a crisp finish. Stored in an airtight box, they will keep you going for days – that is, if they last that long!

1 To make the pastry, put the flours in a bowl with the salt and turmeric. Slowly mix in just enough of the measured water (or a little more, if necessary) to form a soft dough. Knead for 2 minutes, then cover the bowl with clingfilm and leave to rest for 15–20 minutes.

2 To make the filling, toast the sesame seeds in a dry pan over a low heat for 2 minutes, without letting them change colour. Tip the seeds into a bowl. Repeat with the poppy seeds, then with the coconut, then the fennel seeds. Add the remaining filling ingredients to the seeds and coconut and mix well.

3 Divide the dough into 4 portions. Working with each portion in turn, roll it out into a thin circle with a diameter of roughly 22–23 cm (8½–9 inches). Using a pastry brush, dampen the pastry circle with water. Sprinkle a quarter of the filling mixture over it and press down slightly. Roll up the circle like a Swiss roll, then cut crossways into pieces with a thickness of about 15 mm (⅝ inch).

4 Fill a deep-fat fryer or deep, heavy-based saucepan with enough oil for deep-frying and heat it to 170–180°C (340–350°F). Line a plate with some kitchen paper. Working in batches, fry the bhakarwadi for about 2 minutes on each side, until golden brown. Transfer to the paper-lined plate to drain excess oil. Serve hot or cold.

Smashed Alu Tikki

MAKES 8

4 medium potatoes,
  peeled and cut into
  quarters
¾ teaspoon salt
¾ teaspoon chilli
  powder
4 tablespoons
  cornflour
8 tablespoons
  sunflower oil

TO SERVE

150 ml (¼ pint)
  natural yogurt
50 ml (2 fl oz) water
pinch of salt
pinch of chilli powder
pinch of chaat masala
coriander yogurt
  chutney, to taste
tamarind jaggery
  chutney, to taste

Alu tikki is one of the most popular chaats in India and beyond, and it's certainly high up there on my list, too. Often on street corners you can find vendors selling this tikki chaat. They semi-prepare the potato cutlets, half-cooking them in small balls. As soon as you place an order, they turn up the heat, squash the tikkis and fry them until crispy and golden. I usually prepare this dish as a chaat, but you can serve the tikkis without the toppings as a snack or a party canapé.

1 Cook the potatoes in a saucepan of boiling water until cooked through and soft. Drain, set aside in a bowl until cool enough to handle, then mash them with a potato masher. Now add the salt, chilli powder and cornflour to the mash and mix it all well. Divide the mixture into 8 portions and shape them into balls.

2 Heat 2 tablespoons of the oil in a frying pan over a low heat. Add 4 potato balls and cook for 2 minutes on each side until lightly golden. Now add 2 more tablespoons of oil to the pan and, using the back of a large metal or wooden spoon, flatten the balls into flat cakes. Increase the heat to medium and cook for 2 minutes on each side until deep golden brown. Repeat with the remaining 4 potato balls to complete frying the tikkis.

3 Put the yogurt into a bowl, add the measured water and whisk until the mixture is smooth.

4 Place the tikkis on a serving plate and drizzle over the yogurt. Sprinkle the salt, chilli powder and chaat masala on top. Now drizzle over the chutneys and serve immediately.

Gobhi 65

SERVES 4

sunflower oil, for
  deep-frying
1 cauliflower, cut into
  roughly 2.5 cm
  (1 inch) florets

FOR THE BATTER

1 cm (½ inch) piece
  of fresh root ginger,
  peeled and grated
2 tablespoons shop-
  bought chilli-garlic
  sauce
120 g (4¼ oz)
  cornflour
120 g (4¼ oz) rice flour
½ teaspoon salt
230 ml (8 fl oz) water

FOR THE STIR-FRY

2 tablespoons
  sunflower oil
2.5 cm (1 inch) piece
  of fresh root ginger,
  peeled and julienned
8–10 fresh curry leaves
2 tablespoons shop-
  bought chilli-garlic
  sauce
2 tablespoons water

This is my veggie take on the world-famous Indian-restaurant dish known as Chicken 65, the origin of which is hotly debated. Some say it was first served at a restaurant in Chennai where it was number 65 on the menu, while others say it is named after the 65 spices used to make it. Either way, it's delicious! Although my cauliflower version doesn't use 65 spices, I feel it captures something of the flavour of the popular chicken dish.

1 Put all the batter ingredients in a bowl and mix well with a spoon.

2 Heat enough oil for deep-frying in a deep, heavy-based saucepan or deep-fat fryer to 170°C (340°F). (Maintain this throughout cooking.) Dip each cauliflower floret in the batter, then slide it carefully into the hot oil. Cook over a medium heat for a couple of minutes on each side until golden and crispy. Remove the cooked florets with a slotted spoon and transfer to a plate lined with kitchen paper to drain.

3 To make the stir-fry, heat the oil in a separate pan or a wok over a high heat. Add the ginger and curry leaves to the pan and let them sizzle for a minute, then add the chilli-garlic sauce, followed by the measured water. Allow the water to come to the boil, then add the fried cauliflower, stir quickly to cover the florets with the mixture in the pan, then remove from the pan and serve immediately.

Baigan Bhaja

SERVES 4
1 aubergine
½ teaspoon salt
½ teaspoon chilli
  powder
sunflower oil, for
  deep-frying
sea salt flakes
coriander and spinach
  chutney and/or
  tomato chutney,
  to serve

FOR THE BATTER
150 g (5½ oz) gram
  flour (besan)
¾ teaspoon salt
½ teaspoon chilli
  powder
½ teaspoon turmeric
about 300 ml (½ pint)
  water

These pakoras are flavoured with nothing other than salt, turmeric and chilli, yet the flavour is outstanding, no doubt due to the beautifully tender aubergine encased in a crisp, tasty coating. Pair them with coriander and spinach chutney or tomato chutney.

1 Cut the aubergine vertically into thin slices with a thickness of no more than 5 mm (¼ inch). Rub the flesh with the salt and chilli powder then leave to stand for 10 minutes. (This helps to release excess moisture in the aubergine flesh.)

2 To make the batter, combine the gram flour, salt and spices in a bowl, then gradually add just enough of the measured water to form a smooth batter with a thin coating consistency.

3 Heat enough oil for deep-frying in a deep-fat fryer or large, heavy-based saucepan to 190°C (375°F). Line a sheet with some kitchen paper. Working with one slice of aubergine at a time, press it between 2 sheets of kitchen paper to extract excess moisture, then dip the slice in the batter, add it to the hot oil and fry for 1 minute on each side, until deep golden brown and crispy. Transfer to the paper-lined plate and leave to drain excess oil while you fry the remaining aubergine slices. Season with sea salt flakes and serve hot with your preferred chutney.

Dal Papdi Chaat

SERVES 4

FOR THE PAPDI
300 g (10½ oz) plain
  flour, plus extra for
  dusting
½ teaspoon salt
½ teaspoon chilli
  powder
½ teaspoon ground
  cumin
3 tablespoons
  sunflower oil, plus
  extra for deep-frying
120 ml (4 fl oz) water

FOR THE DAL
250 g (9 oz) chana dal
  (split chickpeas)
1 litre (1¾ pints)
  boiling water
1 teaspoon salt
½ teaspoon ground
  turmeric
2 tablespoons ghee
1 green chilli, finely
  chopped
1 teaspoon ground
  cumin
1 teaspoon chaat
  masala

This is one of those dishes that I could happily live off for the rest of my life. The crispness of the papdi with the moreish masala dal and the magical chutneys is the most dreamy combination of all! You can prepare the papdi, dal and chutneys in advance, but put the dish together only when you are ready to eat to retain the satisfying crispiness of the papdi.

1 Start by preparing the papdi. Put the flour, salt, chilli powder, cumin and oil into a bowl and mix well. Slowly add the measured water as you mix with your hand to form a soft dough. Knead the dough for 2 minutes. Cover the bowl with a clean tea towel and leave to rest for 15 minutes.

2 Heat enough oil for deep-frying in a deep, heavy-based saucepan or deep-fat fryer to 170°C (340°F). (Maintain this temperature throughout cooking.)

3 Meanwhile, divide the dough into 4 equal portions and roll out each portion on a lightly floured surface into a thin sheet (in any shape you like) to a depth of roughly 2 mm (⅛ inch). Now cut these sheets into thin strips, diamond shapes or squares. Place the shapes carefully into the hot oil and fry over a medium–low heat for 3–4 minutes until golden and crispy. Remove the papdi from the hot oil using a slotted spoon, transfer to a plate lined with kitchen paper and leave to cool while you prepare the dal.

4 Put the chana dal into a pan with the measured boiling water, salt and turmeric and cook over a medium–low heat for 1 hour until the dal is soft. If it becomes too thick during cooking, stir in another 100 ml (3½ fl oz) boiling water.

TO SERVE
100 ml (3½ fl oz)
   natural yogurt
50 ml (2 fl oz) water
tamarind jaggery
   chutney, to taste
coriander yogurt
   chutney, to taste
pinch of salt
pinch of chilli powder
1 red onion, finely
   chopped
1 green chilli, finely
   chopped

5 Heat the ghee in a small saucepan, then add the chilli. Once the ghee begins to sizzle, take the pan off the heat, add the cumin and chaat masala and mix well. Pour this mixture over the cooked dal and mix well. Leave to cool slightly.

6 When you're ready to serve, put the yogurt into a bowl and stir in the measured water to thin it out.

7 Place the cooled papdis on a plate, top with the warm dal, then drizzle over the yogurt and chutneys. Sprinkle with the salt and chilli powder, then the onion and green chilli. Serve immediately.

Fish Chop

SERVES 4

3 large eggs
300 g (10½ oz)
  skinless cod fillets
1 onion, finely
  chopped
handful of fresh
  coriander leaves,
  finely chopped
2 garlic cloves, finely
  chopped
2 small green chillies,
  finely chopped
½ teaspoon salt
sunflower oil, for
  deep-frying
sea salt flakes
sichuan sauce or
  coriander and
  spinach chutney,
  to serve

FOR THE COATING

2 eggs, lightly beaten
100 g (3½ oz) golden
  breadcrumbs

These delicious fish chops from the streets of Kolkata can be enjoyed hot or cold with a variety of chutneys. If you want something fiery, try them with a sichuan chilli sauce; if you'd prefer something mild, opt for a coriander and spinach chutney.

1 Put the eggs into a small saucepan, cover with water and boil for 10 minutes. Drain and leave to cool, then shell the eggs and mash them in a bowl.

2 In a food processor, blitz the cod to a coarse paste. Add the fish to the mashed eggs, along with the onion, coriander, garlic, chillies and salt. Mix thoroughly so that the flavours are well combined.

3 Shape the mixture into balls the size of a lemon, then press to flatten them slightly. Dip each one in the beaten egg, then roll them in the breadcrumbs until fully coated.

4 Heat enough oil for deep-frying in a deep-fat fryer or a deep, heavy-based saucepan to 170–180°C (340–350°F). Line a plate with some kitchen paper. Fry the chops a few at a time for about 2 minutes, until they are cooked through and golden. Transfer to the paper-lined plate and leave to drain excess oil while you fry the remaining chops.

5 Season with sea salt flakes and serve warm with your choice of sauce or chutney.

Masala Papdi

MAKES 1 PLATEFUL
100 g (3½ oz) plain
flour, plus extra for
dusting
1 tablespoon kasuri
methi (dried
fenugreek leaves)
¼ teaspoon salt
¼ teaspoon carom
seeds (ajwain)
¼ teaspoon garam
masala
¼ teaspoon chilli
powder
¼ teaspoon ground
turmeric
1 tablespoon sunflower
oil, plus extra for
deep-frying
about 45 ml
(3 tablespoons) water

This is the most popular snack in my house. It used to be my favourite snack growing up and now it's my kids' favourite, too. My mum would always keep a box of papdi in the cupboard and refill it as soon as it was empty. I make them often but not as often as she did, as I find they disappear faster than I can make them. No one can ever have just one.

1 Mix all the dry ingredients together in a bowl. Add the 1 tablespoon of oil and rub in with your fingertips until the mixture resembles breadcrumbs. Then gradually add just enough of the water, or a little more if needed, to bring the mixture together into a soft dough. Cover and let it rest for 5 minutes.

2 Divide the dough into 4 portions. Roll out each portion on a lightly floured work surface into a thin sheet about 15–18 cm (6–7 inches) square. Using a sharp knife, cut the sheet into strips about 2.5 cm (1 inch) wide.

3 Heat enough oil for deep-frying in a deep-fat fryer or deep, heavy-based pan (ensuring the pan is no more than one-third full) to about 170°C (340°F). Line a plate with kitchen paper.

4 Deep-fry the pastry strips, in batches, for a few seconds, then turn over and cook until golden. Transfer to the paper-lined plate to absorb the excess oil and cool while you fry the remaining pastry strips. They will crisp up as they cool down.

5 The masala papdi will keep in an airtight container for up to 2 weeks.

Masala Peanuts

60 g (2¼ oz) gram
  flour (besan)
30 g (1 oz) rice flour
20 g (¾ oz) cornflour
1 teaspoon chilli
  powder
½ teaspoon ground
  turmeric
½ teaspoon garlic salt
250 g (9 oz) roasted,
  unsalted peanuts
2 teaspoons sunflower
  oil, plus extra for
  shallow-frying
60 ml (4 tablespoons)
  water

These crispy, spicy and delicious peanuts are a very popular snack in India, where you will find them in all corner shops and sweet shops. They are so easy to make at home, and perfect with a cup of tea or a drink. The only problem is that once you start eating them, it's quite difficult to stop!

1 Mix all the flours and spices together in a bowl, then stir in the peanuts.

2 Add the 2 teaspoons of oil and mix well, then gradually whisk in the water to make a thick gloopy batter that coats the peanuts.

3 Heat enough oil for shallow-frying in a frying pan. Line a plate with kitchen paper.

4 Working in a couple of batches, carefully add the coated peanuts to the hot oil, separating them as you go if you can, and cook over a medium heat for 2–3 minutes until golden and crispy. Transfer to the paper-lined plate to absorb the excess oil and cool while you fry the remaining peanuts. They will crisp up more once they have cooled down.

5 The peanuts will keep in an airtight container for up to 2 weeks.

VEGETABLES

Lentil and Mango Salad

FOR THE SALAD
100 g (3½ oz) moong
  dal (split mung beans)
1 red onion, finely
  chopped
1 cucumber, diced
1 carrot, grated
1 raw green or unripe
  mango, peeled and
  finely chopped

FOR THE TADKA
1 tablespoon rapeseed
  oil
1 teaspoon black
  mustard seeds
1 teaspoon chilli flakes
½ teaspoon salt
1 tablespoon lemon
  juice

You might wonder what lentils are doing in a salad with mangoes, but let me tell you that I was just as surprised when I tried this at my friend Jayashree's house. She often makes it in the summer, when mangoes are in season, and it's quickly become one of my favourites too. Don't worry if you can't find Indian green mangoes – you can use ordinary hard, unripe mangoes from the supermarket instead.

1 Soak the moong dal in a bowl of cold water for 3–4 hours, then drain thoroughly. Return to the bowl with the rest of the salad ingredients.

2 To make the tadka, heat the oil in a small pan and add the mustard seeds. Once they start to sizzle, remove the pan from the heat and add the chilli flakes and salt. Pour this over the salad.

3 Drizzle the salad with the lemon juice, toss it all well and then serve.

4 This will last in the refrigerator for a couple of days.

Beetroot, Carrot and Peanut Salad

FOR THE SALAD

50 g (1¾ oz) roasted
  peanuts
4 uncooked beetroot,
  about 400 g (14 oz),
  grated
1 red onion, finely
  chopped
20 g (¾ oz) fresh
  coriander, finely
  chopped
1 carrot, grated
2 tablespoons lime
  juice
½ teaspoon salt

FOR THE TADKA

1 tablespoon
  groundnut oil
1 teaspoon cumin
  seeds
2 green chillies, finely
  chopped

I was blown away by this salad when my friend Pranoti made it for me – I never would have thought of combining peanuts and beetroot. Even my kids, who don't like beetroot that much, absolutely love this quick dish. It gets so much flavour and crunch from the peanuts and cumin seeds, I think it's a must-have on summer tables.

1 Use a pestle and mortar to coarsely crush the peanuts, then put them into a large bowl with the rest of the salad ingredients.

2 To make the tadka, heat the oil in a small pan and add the cumin seeds. Once they start to sizzle, add the green chillies, give them a stir, then take the pan off the heat. Pour the tadka over the salad, toss well and serve.

3 This will keep in the refrigerator for a couple of days.

Courgette Bharta

SERVES 4

FOR THE
COURGETTES

4 courgettes, about
    800 g (1 lb 12 oz)
1 teaspoon rapeseed oil
¼ teaspoon salt
¼ teaspoon freshly
    ground black pepper

FOR THE BHARTA

1 teaspoon rapeseed oil
1 teaspoon black
    mustard seeds
1 cm (½ inch)
    fresh root ginger,
    peeled and cut into
    matchsticks
¼ teaspoon salt
½ teaspoon chilli
    powder
1 tablespoon lime juice

Usually in India the word 'bharta' describes a roasted aubergine dish, but here I'm making it with courgettes. I was inspired by my friend Abha, who made bharta with potatoes when I visited her home. I wanted to try her recipe with courgettes and found they work beautifully with these simple spices. You can serve this warm, or cold as a salad.

1 Preheat the oven to 200°C (400°F), Gas Mark 6. Slice the courgettes into 5 mm (¼ inch) discs. Put them into a bowl with the oil, salt and pepper and mix well. Spread the slices on a baking tray, making sure they do not overlap, and roast for 10 minutes.

2 To make the bharta, heat the oil in a pan and add the mustard seeds. Once they start to sizzle, add the ginger and let it cook for 1 minute. Add the salt, chilli powder and roast courgette slices and mix well.

3 Squeeze the lime juice over the top, give it a stir and serve. This is best enjoyed immediately but can also be served warm or cold as a salad.

Potato, Paneer and Chickpea Curry

SERVES 4

2 tablespoons
  sunflower oil
2 onions, roughly
  chopped
4 tomatoes, roughly
  chopped
1 small green chilli,
  chopped
2 garlic cloves,
  chopped
2.5 cm (1 inch) piece
  of fresh root ginger,
  peeled and chopped
200 ml (7 fl oz) water
1 cinnamon stick
1½ teaspoons salt
1 teaspoon granulated
  sugar
2 teaspoons garam
  masala
½ teaspoon ground
  turmeric
½ teaspoon chilli
  powder
100 g (3½ oz) paneer,
  cubed
2 floury potatoes,
  boiled, peeled and
  cubed
400 g (14 oz) can
  chickpeas
soft kachori, rice or
  chapattis, to serve

Soft, fluffy potato and cubes of paneer soak up the flavours of the sauce in this light, delicious curry, while the chickpeas add a lovely texture. This dish is very popular in Kolkata and best teamed with soft kachori, but if you want a healthier version, serve it with rice or chapattis.

1 Heat 1 tablespoon of the oil in a saucepan over a medium heat. Add the onions, tomatoes, chilli, garlic and ginger and cook for 10 minutes, or until everything is softened.

2 Transfer the mixture to a blender or food processor, add 100 ml (3½ fl oz) of the measured water and blend to a smooth paste.

3 Heat the remaining oil in a saucepan over a medium heat. Add the cinnamon stick and cook for a few seconds, then stir in the onion and tomato paste. Cover the pan with a lid and cook over a low heat for 10–15 minutes, until well cooked.

4 Add the salt, sugar, spices and the remaining 100 ml (3½ fl oz) measured water to the pan and mix well. Stir in the paneer, potatoes and the chickpeas along with their canning liquid. Cover and cook for about 10 minutes, until the sauce thickens and the potatoes are tender. Serve the curry hot with soft kachori, rice or chapattis.

Tamarind Aubergine Curry

SERVES 2

FOR THE CURRY
1 tablespoon sunflower
   oil
pinch of asafoetida
2 onions, thinly sliced
1 tablespoon fennel
   seeds
1 teaspoon chilli
   powder
1 teaspoon ground
   ginger
200 ml (7 fl oz) water
1 teaspoon sugar
1 teaspoon tamarind
   paste

**FOR THE
AUBERGINE**
1 aubergine, cut into
   fingers 5–7.5 cm
   (2–3 inches) long
¼ teaspoon salt
2–3 tablespoons
   sunflower oil

If you are an aubergine fan, then this dish is sure to become your next favourite thing. The fried aubergine picks up on the aniseed notes of the fennel and the sour kick from the tamarind, and the whole combination is just heavenly. Be careful not to taste it too much along the way, as you might have nothing left to eat at the end! Serve with some rice or paratha.

1 To prepare the aubergine, place it on a plate, sprinkle with the salt and set aside for 10 minutes.

2 Meanwhile, heat the oil for the curry in a pan, add the asafoetida and let it sizzle for a few seconds. Then add the onions and cook over a medium heat for 10 minutes until golden.

3 Heat the oil for the aubergine in a large frying pan. Pat the aubergine fingers dry, add them to the hot oil and cook over a high heat for 2 minutes until golden.

4 While the aubergine is cooking, heat a small frying pan, add the fennel seeds and dry-roast over a low heat for a minute. Then use a pestle and mortar to crush them.

5 Add the crushed fennel seeds to the onions and cook for a minute. Then stir in the ground spices and add the fried aubergine with the measured water. Cook over a low heat for 10 minutes.

6 Stir in the sugar and tamarind and cook over a high heat for 5 minutes until the sauce thickens, then serve.

Mixed Vegetable Curry

SERVES 4

2 tablespoons
  sunflower oil
1 teaspoon cumin
  seeds
1 teaspoon black
  mustard seeds
1 bay leaf
2 onions, finely
  chopped
1 green chilli, finely
  chopped
2 garlic cloves, grated
2.5 cm (1 inch) piece
  of fresh root ginger,
  peeled and grated
1 teaspoon salt
1 teaspoon ground
  turmeric
1 teaspoon chilli
  powder
1 teaspoon garam
  masala
1 teaspoon amchur
  (mango powder)
½ teaspoon sugar
2 tomatoes, finely
  chopped
100 ml (3 ½ fl oz)
  boiling water

We all have those oddments of veg in the refrigerator – a lonely carrot, some peas, the last bit of a cauliflower or half an onion. This recipe is the perfect way to use up all those vegetable leftovers. I have used three different veg here, but you can add a few other ingredients if you have them and make this curry your own. Serve it with some rice or chapattis and a nice raita for a lovely meal.

1 Heat the oil in a pan and add the cumin and mustard seeds and the bay leaf. Once they start to sizzle, add the chopped onions with the green chilli and cook over a medium heat for 10 minutes until golden. Then add the garlic and ginger and cook for a minute.

2 Meanwhile, heat the oil for the vegetables in a large frying pan. Add all of the vegetables and cook them over a medium–high heat for 8–10 minutes until lightly coloured.

2 tablespoons
  sunflower oil
½ cauliflower, cut into
  small florets
2 carrots, cut into
  small pieces
200 g (7 oz) fine green
  beans, cut into 2.5 cm
  (1 inch) pieces

3 Stir the salt, ground spices and sugar into the onions with the tomatoes and cook for a minute. Then add the vegetables and pour in the measured boiling water. Cover and cook over a low–medium heat for 10 minutes until the cauliflower is soft, then serve.

Garlicky Mushroom Sabji

SERVES 4

2 tablespoons
sunflower oil
1 teaspoon fenugreek
seeds
1 onion, thinly sliced
4 garlic cloves, thinly
sliced
600 g (1 lb 5 oz)
chestnut mushrooms,
thinly sliced
100 ml (3 ½ fl oz)
natural yogurt
½ teaspoon salt
1 teaspoon ground
coriander
1 teaspoon ground
cumin
1 teaspoon chilli
powder
handful of chives,
finely chopped

I have made many different mushroom curries over the years, but I wanted to try a new approach. So I devised this mushroom sabji with tons of flavour but without a sauce so that you can scoop it up with some naan or chapattis. Using just a handful of spices and some yogurt, you really can't go wrong with this simple dish. Serve with naan or a dal such as the Spinach and Coconut Dal.

1 Heat the oil in a pan, add the fenugreek seeds and cook over a medium–low heat for a few seconds until they start to change colour. Add the onion and cook over a medium heat for 8–10 minutes until golden. Then add the garlic and cook for a minute.

2 Add the mushrooms and cook over a high heat for 5 minutes, then turn the heat down to low.

3 Mix the yogurt, salt and ground spices together in a bowl, then add to the mushrooms and cook for a minute, stirring constantly to prevent the yogurt from splitting.

4 Cook over a medium heat for 10 minutes until the liquid has almost all cooked off.

5 Add the chives and serve.

Paneer and Purple Sprouting Broccoli Sabji

SERVES 4

1 tablespoon sunflower oil

1 teaspoon mustard seeds

10 curry leaves

2 red onions, finely chopped

225 g (8 oz) paneer, cut into 1 cm (½ inch) dice

225 g (8 oz) purple sprouting broccoli, cut into small chunks

½ teaspoon salt

½ teaspoon ground turmeric

½ teaspoon chilli powder

½ teaspoon amchur (mango powder)

50 ml (2 fl oz) boiling water

If you're thinking that this sounds like an unusual combination then, yes, you are definitely right. But it is one that works a treat. The earthiness of the broccoli goes well with soft, spice-infused paneer. This dish is great served with chapatti, or in a wrap with some spicy chutney, or as a side dish with lentils and rice.

1 Heat the oil in a saucepan over a low heat. Add the mustard seeds and let them sizzle for a few seconds, then mix in the curry leaves and onions and cook over a low heat for 5 minutes, until the onions have softened.

2 Meanwhile, soak the paneer cubes in a bowl of hot water for a minimum of 5 minutes.

3 Stir the broccoli, salt, turmeric, chilli powder, amchur and the measured boiling water (which will create a little steam) into the saucepan. Cover the pan with a lid and cook over a low heat for 5–6 minutes or until the broccoli has softened slightly.

4 Drain the paneer and add it to the saucepan, mixing well. Increase the heat to high and cook for 1 minute, then serve immediately.

New Potato and Tomato Curry

SERVES 4

FOR THE
POTATOES

2–4 tablespoons
rapeseed oil
600 g (1 lb 5 oz) new
potatoes, cut in half

FOR THE CURRY
1 tablespoon rapeseed
oil
pinch of asafoetida
1 teaspoon black
mustard seeds
10 fresh curry leaves
1 green chilli, finely
chopped
1 tablespoon sesame
seeds
2.5 cm (1 inch) piece
of fresh root ginger,
peeled and grated
4 tomatoes, finely
chopped
1 teaspoon salt
1 teaspoon ground
turmeric
1 teaspoon garam
masala
1 teaspoon sugar
200 ml (7 fl oz) boiling
water
juice of ½ lime
20 g (¾ oz) fresh
coriander leaves,
finely chopped

One for the whole family, even the fussy eaters can't say no to this simple curry. The slightly fried potatoes absorb all the amazing heat and sourness from the spices and tomatoes and become juicy and delicious. Use new potatoes in season when available, but otherwise ordinary potatoes cut into small pieces. Enjoy it with fried flatbread, but it's good with rice, too.

1 Heat the oil for the potatoes in a large frying pan. Add the potatoes, cut-side down, in a single layer and cook over a medium–high heat for 1–2 minutes until beautifully golden. You may have to do this in batches, depending on the size of your pan.

2 Meanwhile, start making the curry. Heat the oil in a pan and add the asafoetida. Once it starts to sizzle, add the mustard seeds with the curry leaves and chilli and cook over a low heat until they start to pop. Then add the sesame seeds and ginger and cook for a few seconds.

3 Add the tomatoes and cook over a medium heat for 5 minutes until they start to soften. Stir in the salt, ground spices and sugar and cook for a minute.

4 Add the golden potatoes and the measured boiling water, cover and cook over a low to medium heat for about 10 minutes until the potatoes are cooked through.

5 Add the lime juice and coriander, mix well, then serve.

**FOR THE
MARINADE**

150 ml (¼ pint)
natural yogurt

¼ teaspoon salt

½ teaspoon chilli
powder

¼ teaspoon ground
turmeric

1 teaspoon tandoori
masala

4 Stir the ginger, garlic and green chilli into the onions in
the pan and cook for 1 minute. Now mix in the canned
tomatoes and measured water, cover the pan with a lid
and cook over a low heat for 15 minutes.

5 Add the salt and spices to the pan, followed by the cooked
paneer cubes. Combine well, then stir in the cream and
serve immediately.

Ultimate Potato Sabji

SERVES 4

50 ml (2 fl oz) rapeseed
oil
pinch of asafoetida
1 teaspoon cumin
seeds
1 onion, finely
chopped
2.5 cm (1 inch) piece
of fresh root ginger,
peeled and finely
chopped
4 garlic cloves, finely
chopped
1 green chilli, finely
chopped
4 medium potatoes,
peeled and cut into
2.5 cm (1 inch) dice
½ teaspoon salt
½ teaspoon ground
turmeric
½ teaspoon chaat
masala
1 teaspoon chilli
powder
1 teaspoon garam
masala
1 teaspoon amchur
(mango powder)
handful of fresh
coriander leaves,
finely chopped

At first I was having trouble finding the right name for this
sabji (vegetable dish). It is spicy, moreishly sour and the most
delicious, quick and flavourful potato dish you will ever make.
Then the word 'ultimate' came to mind, because that's what
it is – simply the best potato sabji!

1 Heat the oil in a saucepan over a medium–low heat. Add
the asafoetida and cumin and let the mixture sizzle for
a few seconds, then stir in the onion and cook for 4–5
minutes until softened.

2 Add the ginger, garlic and chilli to the pan, mix well and
continue to cook over a medium–low heat for 1 minute.
Next, stir in the potatoes and cook over a high heat for
1 minute. Now cover the pan with a lid and cook over a
low heat for 10–12 minutes until the potatoes are cooked
through and soft.

3 Add the salt and spices to the pan with the coriander, mix
well and cook over a high heat for 1 minute more, then
serve immediately.

Tandoori Paneer Curry

SERVES 4

450 g (1 lb) paneer, cut
  into 2.5 cm (1 inch)
  cubes

6 tablespoons
  sunflower oil

2 onions, finely
  chopped

2.5 cm (1 inch) piece
  of fresh root ginger,
  peeled and finely
  chopped

4 garlic cloves, finely
  chopped

1 green chilli, finely
  chopped

400 g (14 oz) can
  chopped tomatoes

100 ml (3½ fl oz)
  water

½ teaspoon salt

½ teaspoon ground
  turmeric

1 teaspoon chilli
  powder

1 teaspoon garam
  masala

1 teaspoon tandoori
  masala

3 tablespoons double
  cream

By cooking paneer in tandoori masala with some yogurt and spices, you give it a delicious coating. When you then add the paneer to a tasty curry, you layer flavour upon flavour to make the ultimate dish for paneer-lovers. I have two of those at home – both my kids are big fans of paneer and they love this dish.

1 Put all the marinade ingredients into a large bowl and mix well. Now add the paneer cubes and combine gently to ensure all are coated well. Cover the bowl and leave to marinate for 30 minutes.

2 Heat 4 tablespoons of the oil in a saucepan over a medium–low heat. Add the paneer cubes without crowding them to ensure they cook evenly. Cook for 1 minute, then turn them over and cook for 1 minute more until golden. Leave the paneer to one side.

3 Heat the remaining oil in the same pan and add the onions. Cook these over a medium–low heat for 8–10 minutes until nicely golden.

Ultimate Potato Sabji

SERVES 4

50 ml (2 fl oz) rapeseed
oil

pinch of asafoetida

1 teaspoon cumin
seeds

1 onion, finely
chopped

2.5 cm (1 inch) piece
of fresh root ginger,
peeled and finely
chopped

4 garlic cloves, finely
chopped

1 green chilli, finely
chopped

4 medium potatoes,
peeled and cut into
2.5 cm (1 inch) dice

½ teaspoon salt

½ teaspoon ground
turmeric

½ teaspoon chaat
masala

1 teaspoon chilli
powder

1 teaspoon garam
masala

1 teaspoon amchur
(mango powder)

handful of fresh
coriander leaves,
finely chopped

At first I was having trouble finding the right name for this sabji (vegetable dish). It is spicy, moreishly sour and the most delicious, quick and flavourful potato dish you will ever make. Then the word 'ultimate' came to mind, because that's what it is – simply the best potato sabji!

1 Heat the oil in a saucepan over a medium–low heat. Add the asafoetida and cumin and let the mixture sizzle for a few seconds, then stir in the onion and cook for 4–5 minutes until softened.

2 Add the ginger, garlic and chilli to the pan, mix well and continue to cook over a medium–low heat for 1 minute. Next, stir in the potatoes and cook over a high heat for 1 minute. Now cover the pan with a lid and cook over a low heat for 10–12 minutes until the potatoes are cooked through and soft.

3 Add the salt and spices to the pan with the coriander, mix well and cook over a high heat for 1 minute more, then serve immediately.

Cauliflower Masala

SERVES 4

2 tablespoons
sunflower oil
1 teaspoon fennel
seeds
1 teaspoon cumin
seeds
3 onions, thinly sliced
2.5 cm (1 inch) piece
of fresh root ginger,
peeled and finely
chopped
4 garlic cloves, finely
chopped
1 green chilli, finely
chopped
2 tomatoes, thinly
sliced
1 teaspoon salt
1 teaspoon ground
turmeric
2 teaspoons ground
coriander
1 teaspoon garam
masala
1 teaspoon chilli
powder
1 tablespoon shop-
bought chilli-garlic
sauce
1 cauliflower, cut into
florets
8–10 mint leaves,
finely chopped

This is a stunning veggie dish, yet it's easy to make and ready in a flash! Cauliflower is one of my favourite vegetables. It can be cooked in so many ways and lends itself to all sorts of spicing. For this recipe I add all the flavours from my spice box as well as some chilli-garlic sauce for extra depth. You can use any shop-bought chilli-garlic sauce, but if you don't have any, substitute harissa or a chilli-tomato sauce – either works beautifully.

1 Heat the sunflower oil in a saucepan over a medium– low heat. Add the fennel and cumin seeds and cook for 1–2 minutes until they begin to sizzle. Stir in the onions and cook over a medium–low heat for 8–10 minutes until golden.

2 Add the ginger, garlic and chilli to the saucepan, stir well and cook for 1 minute. Add the tomatoes and mix well. Stir the salt and spices in, then add the chilli-garlic sauce.

3 Finally, add the cauliflower to the saucepan and mix well, then cover the pan with a lid and cook over a medium–low heat for 10–12 minutes until the florets are softened and cooked through. Take the pan off the heat, sprinkle over the mint and serve immediately.

Sour and Spicy Okra with Potatoes

SERVES 4

1 tablespoon sunflower
oil

1 teaspoon cumin
seeds

3 garlic cloves, finely
chopped

2 onions, thinly sliced

1 potato, unpeeled,
thinly sliced

1 teaspoon salt

1 teaspoon garam
masala

1 teaspoon chilli
powder

1 teaspoon chaat
masala

1 tomato, thinly sliced

300 g (10½ oz)
okra, quartered
lengthways

1 teaspoon lemon juice

This is something my mum makes all the time to accompany
dal and chapatti. I do like it that way, but I love to put the
leftovers into a wrap or toastie and serve it with tomato
chutney – a brilliant combination.

1 Heat the oil in a pan over a medium-to-low heat and add
the cumin seeds. Once they begin to sizzle, add the garlic
and cook for a minute, until it is just beginning to colour.
Add the onions and cook for 2 minutes so that they begin
to soften. Now turn the heat to high, add the potato and
cook for 2 minutes.

2 Add the salt, garam masala, chilli powder and chaat
masala, plus the tomato and okra. Cover and cook for 10
minutes over a low heat, until the vegetables are tender.

3 Remove the lid and finish over a high heat for 2 minutes,
to crisp the vegetables slightly. Stir in the lemon juice
and serve.

4 This will keep in an airtight container in the refrigerator
for 4–5 days. Reheat thoroughly before serving.

Tandoori Veg Kebab

MAKES 8

FOR THE BULGUR WHEAT

150 g (5½ oz) bulgur wheat

900 ml (1½ pints) boiling water

1 tablespoon lemon juice

1 tablespoon rapeseed oil

¼ teaspoon salt

¼ teaspoon freshly ground black pepper

FOR THE SKEWERS

1 sweet potato, halved lengthways and cut into 1 cm (½ inch) slices

1 courgette, cut into 5 mm (¼ inch) circles

1 red onion, cut into thin wedges

100 g (3½ oz) natural yogurt

1 tablespoon tandoori masala

¼ teaspoon chilli powder

¼ teaspoon salt

oil, for brushing

You don't really need a barbecue to enjoy these vegetable kebabs. They can also be cooked under a grill or in a frying pan – whatever you have handy. The combination of courgettes, sweet potatoes, red onions and tandoori masala is so simple yet so amazing. I've made this a substantial main course by serving the kebabs with bulgur wheat. You'll find the yogurt dressing adds a lovely finish and flavour.

1 Put the bulgur wheat into a heatproof bowl and cover with the measured boiling water. Leave to soak for 20 minutes, then drain well. (If you are using bamboo skewers, soak them in water now too. You'll need 8 of them.)

2 Wipe out the bowl and return the bulgur to it. Add the lemon juice, oil, salt and pepper, and mix well. Set aside.

3 To prepare the kebabs, par-cook the sliced sweet potato in a pan of boiling water for 2 minutes only. Rinse and drain.

4 Put the courgette and onion into a large bowl and add the sweet potato slices. In a small bowl, mix the yogurt, tandoori masala, chilli powder and salt together and pour this all over the veg. Stir to make sure the veg are well covered with the marinade.

FOR THE DRESSING
100 g (3½ oz) natural
   yogurt
¼ teaspoon ground
   cumin
a pinch of salt

5 Preheat your barbecue or grill. Take the skewers and
   thread the veg on to them as you like. Brush a little oil
   over the top. When the barbecue or grill is hot, cook for
   20 minutes, turning occasionally, until golden.

6 In a small bowl, mix the dressing ingredients. Spread
   the bulgur wheat on a serving platter, lay the skewers on
   top and drizzle over the dressing to serve. These are best
   eaten immediately.

MEAT & FISH

Yogurt Chicken Curry

SERVES 4

200 ml (7 fl oz) natural yogurt

1 teaspoon salt

1 teaspoon garam masala

½ teaspoon ground turmeric

½ teaspoon chilli powder

2 garlic cloves, grated

600 g (1 lb 5 oz) boneless, skinless chicken thighs, cut into 3 cm (1¼ inch) pieces

2 tablespoons sunflower oil

1 teaspoon cumin seeds

2 tomatoes, thinly sliced

20 g (¾ oz) fresh coriander leaves, finely chopped

I have shared other yogurt chicken recipes in my previous books, but this is the easiest version and one of the most delicious ways to cook chicken – and it's my kids' favourite. I have to admit that I usually make this with chicken on the bone, as the bones add flavour to the curry. But it does take a bit more time to cook and I know many people prefer boneless chicken. This is a foolproof curry that works every single time, and you can enjoy it with any flatbreads or rice.

1   Mix the yogurt, salt, spices and garlic together in a bowl. Add the chicken pieces and turn until well coated in the marinade. Let the chicken marinate while you prepare the curry base.

2   Heat the oil in a pan and add the cumin seeds. Once they start to sizzle, add the tomatoes and cook over a medium heat for 5 minutes until they start to soften.

3   Add the marinated chicken with any excess marinade and mix well, then bring to the boil. Cover and cook over a medium–low heat for 15 minutes or until the chicken is cooked through.

4   Sprinkle with the coriander and serve.

Masala Chicken

SERVES 4

50 g (1 ¾ oz) gram
flour (besan)

70 ml (2 ½ fl oz)
natural yogurt

½ teaspoon kala
namak (black salt)

1 teaspoon Kashmiri
chilli powder

1 teaspoon kasuri
methi (dried
fenugreek leaves)

½ teaspoon garam
masala

½ teaspoon ground
cumin

4 boneless, skinless
chicken thighs, cut
into 5 cm (2 inches)
pieces

3 tablespoons
sunflower oil

When I created this dish, I had no idea how it would turn out. But once I had tasted it, I couldn't stop eating it and since then I have been making it a lot when entertaining or cooking for friends. You can also cook it on a hot barbecue or in a hot oven for about 10 minutes until cooked through. This is flavourful enough to serve on its own, although it's great with a ginger and chilli chutney. Just make sure to cook extra; it's devilishly moreish.

1 Heat a frying pan, add the flour and toast over a low heat for about 2 minutes or until it starts to change colour, stirring constantly.

2 Put the toasted flour into a bowl with the yogurt, salt and spices and mix together well. Add the chicken pieces and turn in the marinade until well coated.

3 Heat the oil in a pan. Carefully add the marinated chicken pieces to the hot oil and cook over a medium–low heat for 8–10 minutes, turning halfway through, until golden and cooked through.

Korma-Style Chicken Curry

SERVES 4

2 tablespoons
  sunflower oil
1 cinnamon stick,
  broken up into small
  pieces
2 onions, roughly
  chopped
1 green chilli, roughly
  chopped
2 garlic cloves, roughly
  chopped
2.5 cm (1 inch) piece
  of fresh root ginger,
  peeled and roughly
  chopped
50 g (1¾ oz) cashew
  nuts
1 tablespoon white
  poppy seeds
100 ml (3½ fl oz) water
1 teaspoon salt
1 teaspoon garam
  masala
1 teaspoon chilli powder
200 ml (7 fl oz) boiling
  water
650 g (1 lb 7 oz)
  boneless, skinless
  chicken thighs, cut
  into 5 cm (2 inches)
  pieces
1 tablespoon double
  cream
20 g (¾ oz) fresh
  coriander leaves,
  finely chopped

When you have a chicken korma in a restaurant, it tends to be sweet, sometimes with raisins and quite pale. I am not a big fan of that style of korma and once you have tried my version you may well prefer mine, too. The simple spices used in the sauce lend the chicken a lovely warmth, while you get a beautiful creaminess from the cashews, poppy seeds and onions, resulting in a deliciously delicate curry. Serve with spiced layered flatbread, chapattis or naan, or with rice.

1 Heat the oil in a pan and add the cinnamon. Once it starts to sizzle, add the onions with the green chilli and cook over a medium heat for 5 minutes until they start to colour.

2 Add the garlic, ginger and cashew nuts and cook over a medium heat for 5 minutes until lightly golden. Stir in the poppy seeds and then pour in the measured water.

3 Transfer the mixture to a blender and blitz until smooth, then return to the pan.

4 Stir in the salt, ground spices and measured boiling water, then add the chicken pieces. Cover and cook over a medium heat for 10 minutes until the chicken is cooked through.

5 Add the cream and coriander, then serve.

Cauliflower Masala

SERVES 4

2 tablespoons
  sunflower oil
1 teaspoon fennel
  seeds
1 teaspoon cumin
  seeds
3 onions, thinly sliced
2.5 cm (1 inch) piece
  of fresh root ginger,
  peeled and finely
  chopped
4 garlic cloves, finely
  chopped
1 green chilli, finely
  chopped
2 tomatoes, thinly
  sliced
1 teaspoon salt
1 teaspoon ground
  turmeric
2 teaspoons ground
  coriander
1 teaspoon garam
  masala
1 teaspoon chilli
  powder
1 tablespoon shop-
  bought chilli-garlic
  sauce
1 cauliflower, cut into
  florets
8–10 mint leaves,
  finely chopped

This is a stunning veggie dish, yet it's easy to make and ready in a flash! Cauliflower is one of my favourite vegetables. It can be cooked in so many ways and lends itself to all sorts of spicing. For this recipe I add all the flavours from my spice box as well as some chilli-garlic sauce for extra depth. You can use any shop-bought chilli-garlic sauce, but if you don't have any, substitute harissa or a chilli-tomato sauce – either works beautifully.

1 Heat the sunflower oil in a saucepan over a medium–low heat. Add the fennel and cumin seeds and cook for 1–2 minutes until they begin to sizzle. Stir in the onions and cook over a medium–low heat for 8–10 minutes until golden.

2 Add the ginger, garlic and chilli to the saucepan, stir well and cook for 1 minute. Add the tomatoes and mix well. Stir the salt and spices in, then add the chilli-garlic sauce.

3 Finally, add the cauliflower to the saucepan and mix well, then cover the pan with a lid and cook over a medium–low heat for 10–12 minutes until the florets are softened and cooked through. Take the pan off the heat, sprinkle over the mint and serve immediately.

Sour and Spicy Okra with Potatoes

SERVES 4

1 tablespoon sunflower
  oil
1 teaspoon cumin
  seeds
3 garlic cloves, finely
  chopped
2 onions, thinly sliced
1 potato, unpeeled,
  thinly sliced
1 teaspoon salt
1 teaspoon garam
  masala
1 teaspoon chilli
  powder
1 teaspoon chaat
  masala
1 tomato, thinly sliced
300 g (10½ oz)
  okra, quartered
  lengthways
1 teaspoon lemon juice

This is something my mum makes all the time to accompany dal and chapatti. I do like it that way, but I love to put the leftovers into a wrap or toastie and serve it with tomato chutney – a brilliant combination.

1 Heat the oil in a pan over a medium-to-low heat and add the cumin seeds. Once they begin to sizzle, add the garlic and cook for a minute, until it is just beginning to colour. Add the onions and cook for 2 minutes so that they begin to soften. Now turn the heat to high, add the potato and cook for 2 minutes.

2 Add the salt, garam masala, chilli powder and chaat masala, plus the tomato and okra. Cover and cook for 10 minutes over a low heat, until the vegetables are tender.

3 Remove the lid and finish over a high heat for 2 minutes, to crisp the vegetables slightly. Stir in the lemon juice and serve.

4 This will keep in an airtight container in the refrigerator for 4–5 days. Reheat thoroughly before serving.

Tandoori Veg Kebab

MAKES 8

FOR THE BULGUR WHEAT

150 g (5½ oz) bulgur wheat

900 ml (1½ pints) boiling water

1 tablespoon lemon juice

1 tablespoon rapeseed oil

¼ teaspoon salt

¼ teaspoon freshly ground black pepper

FOR THE SKEWERS

1 sweet potato, halved lengthways and cut into 1 cm (½ inch) slices

1 courgette, cut into 5 mm (¼ inch) circles

1 red onion, cut into thin wedges

100 g (3½ oz) natural yogurt

1 tablespoon tandoori masala

¼ teaspoon chilli powder

¼ teaspoon salt

oil, for brushing

You don't really need a barbecue to enjoy these vegetable kebabs. They can also be cooked under a grill or in a frying pan – whatever you have handy. The combination of courgettes, sweet potatoes, red onions and tandoori masala is so simple yet so amazing. I've made this a substantial main course by serving the kebabs with bulgur wheat. You'll find the yogurt dressing adds a lovely finish and flavour.

1   Put the bulgur wheat into a heatproof bowl and cover with the measured boiling water. Leave to soak for 20 minutes, then drain well. (If you are using bamboo skewers, soak them in water now too. You'll need 8 of them.)

2   Wipe out the bowl and return the bulgur to it. Add the lemon juice, oil, salt and pepper, and mix well. Set aside.

3   To prepare the kebabs, par-cook the sliced sweet potato in a pan of boiling water for 2 minutes only. Rinse and drain.

4   Put the courgette and onion into a large bowl and add the sweet potato slices. In a small bowl, mix the yogurt, tandoori masala, chilli powder and salt together and pour this all over the veg. Stir to make sure the veg are well covered with the marinade.

FOR THE DRESSING
100 g (3½ oz) natural
  yogurt
¼ teaspoon ground
  cumin
a pinch of salt

5 Preheat your barbecue or grill. Take the skewers and thread the veg on to them as you like. Brush a little oil over the top. When the barbecue or grill is hot, cook for 20 minutes, turning occasionally, until golden.

6 In a small bowl, mix the dressing ingredients. Spread the bulgur wheat on a serving platter, lay the skewers on top and drizzle over the dressing to serve. These are best eaten immediately.

MEAT & FISH

Yogurt Chicken Curry

SERVES 4

200 ml (7 fl oz) natural yogurt

1 teaspoon salt

1 teaspoon garam masala

½ teaspoon ground turmeric

½ teaspoon chilli powder

2 garlic cloves, grated

600 g (1 lb 5 oz) boneless, skinless chicken thighs, cut into 3 cm (1¼ inch) pieces

2 tablespoons sunflower oil

1 teaspoon cumin seeds

2 tomatoes, thinly sliced

20 g (¾ oz) fresh coriander leaves, finely chopped

I have shared other yogurt chicken recipes in my previous books, but this is the easiest version and one of the most delicious ways to cook chicken – and it's my kids' favourite. I have to admit that I usually make this with chicken on the bone, as the bones add flavour to the curry. But it does take a bit more time to cook and I know many people prefer boneless chicken. This is a foolproof curry that works every single time, and you can enjoy it with any flatbreads or rice.

1 Mix the yogurt, salt, spices and garlic together in a bowl. Add the chicken pieces and turn until well coated in the marinade. Let the chicken marinate while you prepare the curry base.

2 Heat the oil in a pan and add the cumin seeds. Once they start to sizzle, add the tomatoes and cook over a medium heat for 5 minutes until they start to soften.

3 Add the marinated chicken with any excess marinade and mix well, then bring to the boil. Cover and cook over a medium–low heat for 15 minutes or until the chicken is cooked through.

4 Sprinkle with the coriander and serve.

Masala Chicken

SERVES 4

50 g (1¾ oz) gram
flour (besan)
70 ml (2½ fl oz)
natural yogurt
½ teaspoon kala
namak (black salt)
1 teaspoon Kashmiri
chilli powder
1 teaspoon kasuri
methi (dried
fenugreek leaves)
½ teaspoon garam
masala
½ teaspoon ground
cumin
4 boneless, skinless
chicken thighs, cut
into 5 cm (2 inches)
pieces
3 tablespoons
sunflower oil

When I created this dish, I had no idea how it would turn out. But once I had tasted it, I couldn't stop eating it and since then I have been making it a lot when entertaining or cooking for friends. You can also cook it on a hot barbecue or in a hot oven for about 10 minutes until cooked through. This is flavourful enough to serve on its own, although it's great with a ginger and chilli chutney. Just make sure to cook extra; it's devilishly moreish.

1 Heat a frying pan, add the flour and toast over a low heat for about 2 minutes or until it starts to change colour, stirring constantly.

2 Put the toasted flour into a bowl with the yogurt, salt and spices and mix together well. Add the chicken pieces and turn in the marinade until well coated.

3 Heat the oil in a pan. Carefully add the marinated chicken pieces to the hot oil and cook over a medium–low heat for 8–10 minutes, turning halfway through, until golden and cooked through.

Whole Tandoori-Style Chicken

SERVES 3–4

1 whole chicken,
  around 1.5 kg
  (3 lb 5 oz)

FOR THE FIRST
MARINADE

1 teaspoon salt
1 teaspoon Kashmiri
  chilli powder
10 garlic cloves, finely
  chopped
3–4 cm (1¼–1½
  inches) piece of fresh
  root ginger, peeled
  and finely chopped
4 tablespoons lemon
  juice

FOR THE SECOND
MARINADE

200 ml (7 fl oz)
  natural yogurt
1 tablespoon ground
  coriander
1 tablespoon garam
  masala
2 tablespoons tandoori
  masala powder
1 teaspoon amchur
  (mango powder)
1 teaspoon salt
1 tablespoon mustard
  oil
40 g (1½ oz) fresh
  coriander, leaves and
  stems finely chopped

I have tried and tested this famous dish with various spices over the years and have found this version works perfectly every time. It's cooked in a regular oven rather than a tandoor, but it also works well on the barbecue, which lends the dish an extra smoky flavour. If you prefer, use small cuts of chicken, such as drumsticks or thighs, instead of the whole bird. This dish is great served with salad or pulao.

1 Combine the ingredients for the first marinade in a small bowl and mix well. Rub this all over the chicken, then cover and leave to rest in the refrigerator for 1 hour.

2 Put all the ingredients for the second marinade, except the fresh coriander, into another bowl and mix well. Once combined, stir in the fresh coriander. Rub this mixture under the skin of the chicken, then rub the remainder inside the cavity. Leave to marinate in the refrigerator for 1 hour.

3 Preheat the oven to 180°C (350°F), Gas Mark 4. Put the chicken into a roasting tin and roast for 1 hour 20 minutes, which will give you a perfect tandoori chicken. To check it is done, pierce the thigh with a skewer – the juices should run clear. If not, continue roasting until they do.

4 Transfer the chicken to a serving plate and let it rest for 15 minutes before serving.

Onion and Whole Spice Chicken Curry

SERVES 4

1 tablespoon sunflower
oil

2 bay leaves

1 cinnamon stick

8 black peppercorns

8 cloves

4 green cardamom
pods

6 onions, 3 finely
chopped, 3 quartered

2 small green chillies,
finely chopped

2 garlic cloves, finely
chopped

1 cm (½ inch) piece
of fresh root ginger,
peeled and finely
chopped

2 tablespoons tomato
purée

1 tablespoon ground
coriander

1 teaspoon garam
masala

1 teaspoon ground
turmeric

1 teaspoon salt

100 ml (3½ fl oz)
natural yogurt

100 ml (3½ fl oz)
boiling water

8 skinless chicken
thighs on the bone

This one is my go-to recipe for making the best chicken curry
in the shortest amount of time, with the least amount of effort!
It will soon be your favourite, too – the spices work their
magic on the chicken, and the generous use of onions gives
the dish a delicious flavour. Despite the fact that it's on my
list of all-time top comfort foods, this meal is very healthy.
Serve it with rice or chapatti.

1 Heat the oil in a saucepan over a medium–low heat. Once
   hot, add the bay leaves, cinnamon, peppercorns, cloves
   and cardamom and let them sizzle for a few seconds.
   Stir in the finely chopped onions and chillies and cook
   until the onions are golden brown – this might take
   20–25 minutes.

2 Add the garlic and ginger to the saucepan and mix well.
   Continue to cook for 2 minutes, then stir in the tomato
   purée and cook for 2 minutes more. Now mix in the
   coriander, garam masala, turmeric and salt and cook for
   another minute.

3 Stir the yogurt into the saucepan along with the measured
   boiling water, then add the chicken and the quartered
   onions. Cover the pan with a lid and simmer gently for
   40–45 minutes or until the chicken is cooked through.
   Serve immediately.

Coconut Chicken Curry

SERVES 4
1 ½ tablespoons
  sunflower oil
1 teaspoon mustard
  seeds
10 curry leaves
2 onions, thinly sliced
2 green chillies, thinly
  sliced
4 garlic cloves, finely
  chopped
1 cm (½ inch) piece
  of fresh root ginger,
  peeled and finely
  chopped
1 teaspoon salt
1 teaspoon ground
  turmeric
1 teaspoon ground
  coriander
½ teaspoon ground
  cinnamon
8 skinless chicken
  pieces on the bone
  (I use 4 thighs and 4
  drumsticks)
400 ml (14 fl oz) can
  coconut milk

So different to the heavily spiced chicken curries you may have tried, this dish has a delicate and refreshing flavour that's best enjoyed with rice rather than bread. The light spicing works beautifully with the coconut milk, and using chicken on the bone adds extra flavour. Don't save this luxurious-tasting curry for the weekend – being quick to make, it's a great choice for midweek meals.

1 Heat the oil in a saucepan over a medium–low heat. Stir in the mustard seeds and cook for 1–2 minutes, until they start to sizzle. Now mix in the curry leaves and, after 1 minute, add the onions and green chillies. Reduce the heat to low and cook for 5–6 minutes, until the onions have softened. Stir in the garlic and ginger and cook for another 2 minutes.

2 Add the salt and spices to the saucepan and mix well. Cook for 1 minute, then stir in the chicken, increase the heat to high and cook for 5 minutes, until the chicken is sealed.

3 Stir in the coconut milk, then cover the pan with a lid, reduce the heat to low and cook for 35–40 minutes, until the chicken is cooked through. Serve immediately.

Chicken Seekh Kebabs

SERVES 8

500 g (1 lb 2 oz)
  skinless chicken
  breast fillets
4 garlic cloves
1 cm (½ inch) piece
  of fresh root ginger,
  peeled
2 small green chillies
30 g (1 oz) fresh
  coriander
1 red onion, roughly
  chopped
¾ teaspoon salt
1 teaspoon Kashmiri
  chilli powder
½ teaspoon garam
  masala
½ teaspoon chaat
  masala
¼ teaspoon freshly
  ground black pepper
30 g (1 oz) Cheddar
  cheese, finely grated
2 tablespoons
  sunflower oil

These beautifully spiced and herby kebabs are great cooked over a barbecue, but can also be done in an oven or on a griddle pan, which is how I usually cook them. And you can shape the mixture into burgers to serve in a bun, if you prefer. Whatever shape or method you choose, the result will be the same – tender and delectable. Serve them on their own, or in a chapatti with chutney and salad.

1 If using bamboo skewers, soak 8 skewers in water for 30 minutes prior to cooking.

2 Using a food processor, break down the chicken breasts to a smooth paste, then tip the paste into a bowl.

3 Now put the garlic, ginger, chillies, coriander and onion into the bowl of the food processor and pulse to roughly chop and combine them. Add this mixture, along with the salt, dried spices, pepper and grated cheese, to the bowl with the minced chicken and mix thoroughly.

red onion slices
2 tablespoons chopped
   fresh coriander
chilli flakes
lime wedges
natural yogurt
   sprinkled with
   toasted cumin seeds

4 Divide the mixture into 8 equal portions. Press 1 portion around a skewer, then roll it between your hands to give it a somewhat cylindrical shape and extend it along the skewer. Keep a bowl of water nearby to dip your hands into between shaping each skewer, as this makes it easier to handle the somewhat sticky mixture. Place the prepared skewer on a tray or chopping board and repeat the process with the remaining portions of the chicken mixture and skewers. If necessary, you can leave the kebabs to rest in the refrigerator for up to 24 hours until you are ready to cook.

5 Heat the oil in a griddle pan. Cook the kebabs over a medium–low heat for 8–10 minutes, turning halfway, until cooked through. Serve immediately with the red onion slices, chopped coriander, chilli flakes, lime wedges to squeeze over and cumin yogurt, if liked.

Chicken Chop

MAKES 20

1 tablespoon sunflower oil, plus extra for deep-frying

1 onion, finely chopped

1 small green chilli, finely chopped

2 garlic cloves, finely chopped

2.5 cm (1 inch) piece of fresh root ginger, peeled and finely chopped

1 teaspoon salt

½ teaspoon ground coriander

½ teaspoon ground cumin

1 teaspoon garam masala

500 g (1 lb 2 oz) minced chicken

2 boiled potatoes, peeled and mashed

handful of fresh coriander leaves, finely chopped

2 eggs, lightly beaten

100 g (3 ½ oz) golden breadcrumbs

coriander and spinach or tomato chutney, to serve

I really enjoyed eating these delicious hot snacks in Kolkata and was fascinated to see that the chefs give each flavour of chop a different shape – egg chops are oval, fish chops, cylindrical, and chicken chops are flat. It makes it very easy to tell them apart.

1 Heat the 1 tablespoon sunflower oil in a saucepan over a medium heat. Add the onion and chilli and cook for 5 minutes, until the onion softens. Add the garlic and ginger and cook for 2 minutes, then add the salt and spices and mix well. Stir in the minced chicken and remove the pan from the heat – you don't want to cook the chicken at this stage or it will not bind well.

2 Transfer the chicken mixture to a bowl. Add the mashed potatoes and coriander and mix well.

3 Divide the chicken mixture into 20 portions. Take 1 portion in your palm and shape it into an oval. Press gently to flatten it a little. Dip the patty in the beaten egg, then roll it in breadcrumbs until coated. Repeat until you've used up all the chicken mixture.

4 Fill a deep-fat fryer or large, heavy-based saucepan with enough oil for deep-frying. Slowly heat the oil to 190°C (375°F). Line a plate with some kitchen paper. When the oil is hot, fry the chicken chops, a few at a time, for 2–3 minutes, turning halfway through, until golden brown. Transfer to the paper-lined plate and leave to drain excess oil while you cook the remaining chicken chops. Serve hot with chutney.

Fish Fry

SERVES 2–4

½ teaspoon salt

½ teaspoon ground turmeric

¼ teaspoon chilli powder

1 medium sea bream, cleaned, gutted and cut into 6 pieces

2 handfuls of fresh coriander leaves, finely chopped

4 garlic cloves, finely chopped

2 small green chillies, finely chopped

4 tablespoons mustard oil

2 tablespoons lemon juice

This crispy, flavourful fried fish dish is a staple in Kolkata, where it's an essential part of the local thali and is eaten with lentils, potato and rice as a main meal, but it also makes a great snack. Coriander and garlic balance the peppery taste of the mustard oil in which the fish is fried.

1 Mix the salt, turmeric and chilli powder in a small bowl. Rub the spice mixture over the fish pieces, then put them into a bowl and leave to stand for 15 minutes.

2 Using a pestle and mortar, mash the coriander, garlic and green chilli to a paste. Smear it over the fish.

3 Heat the mustard oil in a frying pan set over medium heat. Just as it begins to smoke, add the fish pieces and cook for 2–3 minutes on each side, until golden and crisp. Sprinkle over the lemon juice. Serve immediately.

Amritsar-Style Fish

SERVES 4
sunflower oil, for
  shallow-frying
1 trout, about 400–
  500 g (14 oz–1 lb
  2 oz), cleaned, gutted
  and cut into 8 steaks
  about 1 cm (½ inch)
  thick

FOR THE BATTER
50 g (1¾ oz) gram
  flour (besan)
35 g (1¼ oz) plain
  flour
35 g (1¼ oz) cornflour
2 garlic cloves, grated
2.5 cm (1 inch) piece
  of fresh root ginger,
  peeled and grated
1 teaspoon carom
  seeds (ajwain)
½ teaspoon salt
½ teaspoon chilli
  powder
½ teaspoon ground
  turmeric
about 150 ml (¼ pint)
  water

TO SERVE
lime wedges
sliced red onion
chilli flakes

There are many delicious ways in which fish is cooked in Amritsar in North India, and when I visited the city a few years ago I fell in love with the local food. This recipe is inspired by a dish I ate there in a dhabba (small street-side restaurant), and even though it is simple, it's still so delicious. If you can't find trout, then feel free to use any other firm white fish. This is great served with some coriander chutney.

1 To make the batter, mix together all the ingredients except the measured water in a bowl. Then gradually whisk in enough of the water to make a smooth batter with a coating consistency.

2 Heat enough oil for shallow-frying in a frying pan. Line a plate with kitchen paper.

3 Wash the fish pieces and pat them dry. Dip one piece at a time into the batter and then carefully add to the hot oil. Cook over a medium–low heat for 2–3 minutes on each side until golden and cooked through. Transfer to the paper-lined plate to absorb the excess oil.

4 Serve with lime wedges and sliced red onion, sprinkled with chilli flakes.

Tamarind Fish Curry

SERVES 4

700 g (1 lb 9 oz) cod
   fillet, cut into 2–3 cm
   (¾–1¼ inch) pieces
¼ teaspoon salt
¼ teaspoon ground
   turmeric
fresh coconut, very
   finely chopped, to
   garnish (optional)

FOR THE SAUCE
1 tablespoon mustard
   oil
1 teaspoon mustard
   seeds
10 curry leaves
3 shallots, ground to
   a paste using a mini
   food processor
1 teaspoon fresh root
   ginger paste (made
   using a mini food
   processor or pestle
   and mortar)
1 teaspoon garlic paste
   (made using a mini
   food processor or
   pestle and mortar)
1 teaspoon ground
   coriander
½ teaspoon ground
   turmeric
½ teaspoon salt
1 tablespoon tamarind
   paste
400 ml (14 fl oz) can
   coconut milk

Cooking fish is such a joy – it's often a quick and easy job, and you can get so many different results from the same species. The layers of flavour in this curry are wonderful. The simple sauce is quick to produce, but it combines with the fish into something really special. Serve this dish with rice.

1 Put the cod into a large bowl and rub the pieces with the salt and turmeric. Cover the bowl with clingfilm and refrigerate until the curry sauce is almost ready.

2 To make the curry sauce, heat the oil in a saucepan over a medium heat. When it is smoking hot, add the mustard seeds and curry leaves. After 1–2 minutes, once they start to pop, stir in the shallot paste and cook for 3–5 minutes, until golden. Add the ginger and garlic pastes and cook for 1 minute, then stir in the coriander, turmeric and salt. Once combined, add the tamarind paste and coconut milk. Mix well, then cover the pan with a lid and cook for 8–10 minutes, until the sauce has thickened slightly.

3 Add the fish pieces to the sauce and cook gently for 3–4 minutes, until the fish is cooked through. Garnish with the fresh coconut, if liked, and serve immediately.

Fish and Lentil Curry

SERVES 4

2 tablespoons rapeseed
oil

1 teaspoon black
mustard seeds

1 large red onion,
finely chopped

2.5 cm (1 inch) piece
of fresh root ginger,
peeled and grated

2 tomatoes, finely
chopped

1 teaspoon salt

2 teaspoons curry
powder

1 teaspoon ground
turmeric

1 teaspoon chilli
powder

150 g (5½ oz) masoor
dal (split red lentils)

400 ml (14 fl oz) can
coconut milk

100 ml (3½ fl oz)
boiling water

400 g (14 oz) skinless
hake fillet or any
firm white fish, cut
into pieces 7.5 cm
(3 inches) long

chopped chives, to
serve

Fish in any curry is delicious but when cooked with lentils it makes for a wonderfully creamy and hearty dish. I asked my fishmonger which fish he suggested I cook in this curry and he gave me this lovely hake. It worked a treat, but any other firm white fish fillet would be lovely. Serve with Vegetable Pulao or plain rice.

1   Heat the oil in a pan and add the mustard seeds. Once they start to sizzle, add the onion and cook over a medium heat for 5 minutes until softened and starting to change colour. Then add the ginger and cook for a minute.

2   Add the tomatoes and cook over a medium heat for 2 minutes until they start to soften.

3   Stir in the salt and ground spices and then the lentils. Pour in the coconut milk followed by the measured boiling water. Cover and cook over a low–medium heat for 10 minutes until the lentils are soft.

4   Place the fish pieces in the lentils, cover again and cook over a medium heat for 5 minutes until the fish is just cooked through.

5   Sprinkle with chopped chives and serve.

Tandoori Pan-Fried Sea Bream

SERVES 2
1 whole sea bream
(500 g–600 g/ 1 lb
2 oz–1 lb 5 oz)
100 ml (3 ½ fl oz)
natural yogurt
1 cm (½ inch) piece
of fresh root ginger,
peeled and finely
chopped
1 tablespoon tandoori
masala powder
½ teaspoon chilli
powder
½ teaspoon salt
40 g (1 ½ oz) fresh
coriander, leaves and
stems finely chopped
2 teaspoons mustard
oil

FOR THE GARNISH
handful of fresh
coriander leaves
1 large red chilli, sliced
3 limes, halved or
quartered, for
squeezing over

The spices, fresh herbs and yogurt in this dish make it next-level tasty. When you are short on time but still want to cook up a feast, this dish is the best thing you can try – it could not be any simpler! The bream is good-looking enough to sit in the middle of any dining table, and is great served with salads, rice, bread or even on its own.

1 First, score 2 cuts across each side of the fish. Place it in a large dish.

2 In a bowl, combine the yogurt, ginger, tandoori masala, chilli powder, salt, coriander and 1 teaspoon of the mustard oil. Mix well, then spoon some of the mixture into the cavity of the fish. Spread the remainder over the outside of the fish. Leave to rest in the refrigerator for 10 minutes.

3 Heat the remaining mustard oil in a large frying pan over a medium heat. Once it is smoking hot, carefully lay the fish in the pan and cook for 5–6 minutes on each side or until the fish is cooked through and flaky.

4 Serve immediately on a large plate garnished with the coriander leaves, chilli slices and lime pieces.

Hot and Spicy Coconut Prawns

12 raw king prawns,
  shelled and deveined

FOR THE DRY RUB
1 cm (½ inch) piece
  of fresh root ginger,
  peeled and grated
2 garlic cloves, grated
¼ teaspoon salt
¼ teaspoon chilli
  powder
¼ teaspoon ground
  turmeric
¼ teaspoon crushed
  fennel seeds

FOR THE MASALA
1 tablespoon sunflower
  oil
10 curry leaves
½ teaspoon black
  mustard seeds
½ teaspoon fennel seeds
2 small green chillies,
  thinly sliced
2 red onions, thinly
  sliced
100 g (3½ oz) fresh
  coconut, thinly sliced

I'm warning you – this is a hot one! But, of course, you can reduce the quantity of chillies to suit your taste. The fresh prawns and big pieces of coconut are a match made in heaven. Curry leaves and fennel seeds also help to give this dish a unique flavour. Perhaps best of all, it comes together in minutes, making this a great quick-meal option. Serve it with some plain rice or pulao.

1 Put the prawns into a bowl with all the dry rub ingredients and rub them thoroughly over the prawns. Cover the bowl and leave to rest in the refrigerator for 15 minutes while you prepare the masala.

2 Heat the oil in a large saucepan over a medium heat. Add the curry leaves and the mustard and fennel seeds and let them sizzle for a few seconds. Now stir in the green chillies and onions and cook for 2–3 minutes, until they begin to soften.

150 ml (¼ pint)
   boiling water
½ teaspoon salt
½ teaspoon ground
   turmeric
½ teaspoon garam
   masala
1 teaspoon ground
   coriander
1 tablespoon Kashmiri
   chilli powder

3 Add the coconut to the saucepan along with the measured boiling water. Stir well, then cover the pan with a lid and cook for 10 minutes, until the coconut is slightly softer.

4 Next, add the salt, spices and prawns to the pan and mix gently. Increase the heat to high and cook for 5–6 minutes, until the prawns have turned pink and are cooked through. Serve immediately.

Egg and Cabbage Curry

SERVES 4

FOR THE CURRY

2 tablespoons rapeseed
  oil
2 dried bay leaves
2 onions, thinly sliced
½ hispi cabbage,
  about 200 g (7 oz),
  thinly sliced
1 teaspoon sugar
1 teaspoon salt
1 teaspoon chilli
  powder
1 teaspoon garam
  masala
½ teaspoon ground
  turmeric
200 ml (7 fl oz) boiling
  water

FOR THE EGGS

8 eggs
4 tablespoons double
  cream
2 tablespoons rapeseed
  oil

You may not have expected to find a recipe for egg curry in this chapter. I've put it here because many Hindus in India (most of whom are vegetarian) consider eggs to be a form of meat. There are so many ways of making this irresistible curry and I have shared a few versions of it over the years. The addition of cabbage in this recipe gives it a lovely texture and the egg yolks contribute an extra layer of flavour to the sauce. Serve with rice or spiced layered flatbread.

1 To make the curry, heat the oil in a pan, add the bay leaves and onions and cook over a high heat for about 5 minutes. Then add the cabbage and sugar and cook over a medium heat for 10 minutes until the vegetables are soft and golden. Stir in the salt and spices and cook for a minute.

2 While the curry is cooking, put the eggs in a pan, cover with boiling water and cook for 10 minutes. Drain, cool under cold running water and shell them. Cut the eggs in half and separate the egg whites and yolks. Mash the egg yolks with the cream in a bowl. Heat the oil in a pan and fry the egg whites for a couple of minutes until golden.

3 Add the mashed yolks, fried egg whites and measured boiling water to the curry. Cover and cook over a medium heat for 5 minutes until everything has come together, then serve.

DALS

Dal Fry

FOR THE DAL

150 g (5½ oz) toor dal
(split pigeon peas)
50 g (1¾ oz) moong
dal (split mung
beans)
50 g (1¾ oz) chana dal
(split chickpeas)
1 litre (1¾ pints)
boiling water
1 teaspoon salt
1 teaspoon ground
turmeric

**FOR THE FIRST
TADKA**

1 tablespoon ghee
1 tablespoon sunflower
oil
1 teaspoon cumin
seeds
2 garlic cloves, finely
chopped
1 cm (½ inch) piece
of fresh root ginger,
peeled and finely
chopped
1 green chilli, finely
chopped
1 onion, finely
chopped
handful of fresh
coriander leaves,
finely chopped

You might have seen this dal dish on the menu of your local takeaway, and it's just as popular in India, where it is served at dhabas (small roadside eateries). What makes it so delicious is the double tadka – one is stirred through the cooked lentils and the other sits on top of the final dish, waiting for you to break into it and enjoy this delicious combination of three lentils.

1 To make the dal, put all three types of lentils into a saucepan and cover with the measured boiling water. Leave to soak for 1 hour. Stir in the salt and turmeric and cook over a medium–low heat for 40–45 minutes until the lentils are soft and mushy.

2 Make the first tadka towards the end of the cooking time for the dal. Heat the ghee and oil in a saucepan over a medium–low heat and add the cumin seeds. Once they begin to sizzle, add the garlic, ginger, chilli and onion and cook for 5–6 minutes until the onion begins to turn golden. Stir in the chopped coriander and mix well, then pour the tadka over the cooked dal in the saucepan and mix it in well. Transfer the dal to a serving bowl.

FOR THE SECOND TADKA

2 tablespoons ghee

2 garlic cloves, thinly
  sliced

4 red chillies, thinly
  sliced

8–10 fresh curry leaves

3 Now make the second tadka. Heat the ghee over a medium–low heat in the same pan you used to make the first tadka. Add the garlic and chillies and cook for a minute until they soften. Now mix in the curry leaves and let the tadka sizzle for a few seconds, then pour it over the dal and serve immediately.

Cumin Dal

SERVES 4

FOR THE LENTILS
300 g (10½ oz) moong dal (split mung beans)
1.2 litres (2 pints) water
1 teaspoon salt
½ teaspoon ground turmeric

FOR THE TADKA
1 tablespoon ghee
1 teaspoon cumin seeds
2 small green chillies, halved
10 fresh curry leaves
20 g (¾ oz) fresh coriander leaves, finely chopped

Turn to this when you're short on time and need something healthy, delicious and comforting. Moong dal takes very little time to cook and needs only the simplest tempering to make it perfect. I would happily eat this as a bowl of soup, but my kids love it with yogurt and chapatti.

1   Put the dal, measured water, salt and turmeric into a deep pan and bring to the boil. Simmer on a low heat for 20 minutes, until the lentils are soft and mushy.

2   To make the tadka, in a small pan, melt the ghee and add the cumin seeds. Once they start to sizzle, add the green chillies and curry leaves, then, a few seconds later, the coriander.

3   Immediately pour the tadka over the lentils and serve.

4   This will keep in an airtight container in the refrigerator for 4–5 days. Reheat before serving.

Masala Urad Dal

SERVES 4

250 g (9 oz) urad dal
(whole black lentils)
1 litre (1 ¼ pints)
water
1 teaspoon salt
1 teaspoon ground
turmeric
1 tablespoon ghee
1 teaspoon cumin
seeds
a pinch of asafoetida
1 onion, finely
chopped
1 cm (½ inch) fresh
ginger, peeled and
finely chopped
2 garlic cloves, finely
chopped
1 green chilli, finely
chopped
2 tomatoes, finely
chopped
20 g (¾ oz) fresh
coriander leaves,
finely chopped
¼ teaspoon freshly
ground black pepper

This particular dal is a bit different from the others as it is quite thick, which is why it's usually served with flatbreads such as naan or chapatti rather than rice. My mum used to serve it with crispy hot parathas and raita on the side.

1 Put the dal and measured water into a pan and leave to soak for 2 hours.

2 Add the salt and turmeric to the dal and bring to the boil. Cover and cook over a low heat for 35–40 minutes, until very soft – there won't be much liquid left by the time the lentils are done.

3 In a separate pan, heat the ghee and add the cumin seeds. Once they start to sizzle, add the asafoetida and onion and cook for 10 minutes over a medium heat until deep golden brown. Next, add the ginger, garlic and green chilli and cook for another 2 minutes.

4 Add the chopped tomatoes and cook for 5 minutes, until softened. Throw in the coriander and black pepper and mix well.

5 Tip the cooked dal into the onion and tomato mixture and serve warm.

6 Store in an airtight container in the refrigerator for 4–5 days and reheat before serving.

Masala Urad Dal

250 g (9 oz) urad dal
(whole black lentils)
1 litre (1¼ pints)
water
1 teaspoon salt
1 teaspoon ground
turmeric
1 tablespoon ghee
1 teaspoon cumin
seeds
a pinch of asafoetida
1 onion, finely
chopped
1 cm (½ inch) fresh
ginger, peeled and
finely chopped
2 garlic cloves, finely
chopped
1 green chilli, finely
chopped
2 tomatoes, finely
chopped
20 g (¾ oz) fresh
coriander leaves,
finely chopped
¼ teaspoon freshly
ground black pepper

This particular dal is a bit different from the others as it is quite thick, which is why it's usually served with flatbreads such as naan or chapatti rather than rice. My mum used to serve it with crispy hot parathas and raita on the side.

1 Put the dal and measured water into a pan and leave to soak for 2 hours.

2 Add the salt and turmeric to the dal and bring to the boil. Cover and cook over a low heat for 35–40 minutes, until very soft – there won't be much liquid left by the time the lentils are done.

3 In a separate pan, heat the ghee and add the cumin seeds. Once they start to sizzle, add the asafoetida and onion and cook for 10 minutes over a medium heat until deep golden brown. Next, add the ginger, garlic and green chilli and cook for another 2 minutes.

4 Add the chopped tomatoes and cook for 5 minutes, until softened. Throw in the coriander and black pepper and mix well.

5 Tip the cooked dal into the onion and tomato mixture and serve warm.

6 Store in an airtight container in the refrigerator for 4–5 days and reheat before serving.

Cumin Dal

SERVES 4

FOR THE LENTILS
300 g (10½ oz) moong
  dal (split mung beans)
1.2 litres (2 pints)
  water
1 teaspoon salt
½ teaspoon ground
  turmeric

FOR THE TADKA
1 tablespoon ghee
1 teaspoon cumin
  seeds
2 small green chillies,
  halved
10 fresh curry leaves
20 g (¾ oz) fresh
  coriander leaves,
  finely chopped

Turn to this when you're short on time and need something healthy, delicious and comforting. Moong dal takes very little time to cook and needs only the simplest tempering to make it perfect. I would happily eat this as a bowl of soup, but my kids love it with yogurt and chapatti.

1 Put the dal, measured water, salt and turmeric into a deep pan and bring to the boil. Simmer on a low heat for 20 minutes, until the lentils are soft and mushy.

2 To make the tadka, in a small pan, melt the ghee and add the cumin seeds. Once they start to sizzle, add the green chillies and curry leaves, then, a few seconds later, the coriander.

3 Immediately pour the tadka over the lentils and serve.

4 This will keep in an airtight container in the refrigerator for 4–5 days. Reheat before serving.

2 tablespoons ghee
2 garlic cloves, thinly
 sliced
4 red chillies, thinly
 sliced
8–10 fresh curry leaves

3 Now make the second tadka. Heat the ghee over a medium–
low heat in the same pan you used to make the first tadka.
Add the garlic and chillies and cook for a minute until
they soften. Now mix in the curry leaves and let the tadka
sizzle for a few seconds, then pour it over the dal and
serve immediately.

Dal Fry

SERES 4

FOR THE DAL

150 g (5½ oz) toor dal
(split pigeon peas)
50 g (1¾ oz) moong
  dal (split mung
  beans)
50 g (1¾ oz) chana dal
  (split chickpeas)
1 litre (1¾ pints)
  boiling water
1 teaspoon salt
1 teaspoon ground
  turmeric

**FOR THE FIRST
TADKA**

1 tablespoon ghee
1 tablespoon sunflower
  oil
1 teaspoon cumin
  seeds
2 garlic cloves, finely
  chopped
1 cm (½ inch) piece
  of fresh root ginger,
  peeled and finely
  chopped
1 green chilli, finely
  chopped
1 onion, finely
  chopped
handful of fresh
  coriander leaves,
  finely chopped

You might have seen this dal dish on the menu of your local takeaway, and it's just as popular in India, where it is served at dhabas (small roadside eateries). What makes it so delicious is the double tadka – one is stirred through the cooked lentils and the other sits on top of the final dish, waiting for you to break into it and enjoy this delicious combination of three lentils.

1 To make the dal, put all three types of lentils into a saucepan and cover with the measured boiling water. Leave to soak for 1 hour. Stir in the salt and turmeric and cook over a medium–low heat for 40–45 minutes until the lentils are soft and mushy.

2 Make the first tadka towards the end of the cooking time for the dal. Heat the ghee and oil in a saucepan over a medium–low heat and add the cumin seeds. Once they begin to sizzle, add the garlic, ginger, chilli and onion and cook for 5–6 minutes until the onion begins to turn golden. Stir in the chopped coriander and mix well, then pour the tadka over the cooked dal in the saucepan and mix it in well. Transfer the dal to a serving bowl.

DALS

Egg and Cabbage Curry

SERVES 4

FOR THE CURRY
2 tablespoons rapeseed
   oil
2 dried bay leaves
2 onions, thinly sliced
½ hispi cabbage,
   about 200 g (7 oz),
   thinly sliced
1 teaspoon sugar
1 teaspoon salt
1 teaspoon chilli
   powder
1 teaspoon garam
   masala
½ teaspoon ground
   turmeric
200 ml (7 fl oz) boiling
   water

FOR THE EGGS
8 eggs
4 tablespoons double
   cream
2 tablespoons rapeseed
   oil

You may not have expected to find a recipe for egg curry in this chapter. I've put it here because many Hindus in India (most of whom are vegetarian) consider eggs to be a form of meat. There are so many ways of making this irresistible curry and I have shared a few versions of it over the years. The addition of cabbage in this recipe gives it a lovely texture and the egg yolks contribute an extra layer of flavour to the sauce. Serve with rice or spiced layered flatbread.

1 To make the curry, heat the oil in a pan, add the bay leaves and onions and cook over a high heat for about 5 minutes. Then add the cabbage and sugar and cook over a medium heat for 10 minutes until the vegetables are soft and golden. Stir in the salt and spices and cook for a minute.

2 While the curry is cooking, put the eggs in a pan, cover with boiling water and cook for 10 minutes. Drain, cool under cold running water and shell them. Cut the eggs in half and separate the egg whites and yolks. Mash the egg yolks with the cream in a bowl. Heat the oil in a pan and fry the egg whites for a couple of minutes until golden.

3 Add the mashed yolks, fried egg whites and measured boiling water to the curry. Cover and cook over a medium heat for 5 minutes until everything has come together, then serve.

150 ml (¼ pint)
  boiling water
½ teaspoon salt
½ teaspoon ground
  turmeric
½ teaspoon garam
  masala
1 teaspoon ground
  coriander
1 tablespoon Kashmiri
  chilli powder

3 Add the coconut to the saucepan along with the measured
   boiling water. Stir well, then cover the pan with a lid and
   cook for 10 minutes, until the coconut is slightly softer.

4 Next, add the salt, spices and prawns to the pan and
   mix gently. Increase the heat to high and cook for
   5–6 minutes, until the prawns have turned pink and are
   cooked through. Serve immediately.

Hot and Spicy Coconut Prawns

SERVES 4
12 raw king prawns,
  shelled and deveined

FOR THE DRY RUB
1 cm (½ inch) piece
  of fresh root ginger,
  peeled and grated
2 garlic cloves, grated
¼ teaspoon salt
¼ teaspoon chilli
  powder
¼ teaspoon ground
  turmeric
¼ teaspoon crushed
  fennel seeds

FOR THE MASALA
1 tablespoon sunflower
  oil
10 curry leaves
½ teaspoon black
  mustard seeds
½ teaspoon fennel seeds
2 small green chillies,
  thinly sliced
2 red onions, thinly
  sliced
100 g (3½ oz) fresh
  coconut, thinly sliced

I'm warning you – this is a hot one! But, of course, you can reduce the quantity of chillies to suit your taste. The fresh prawns and big pieces of coconut are a match made in heaven. Curry leaves and fennel seeds also help to give this dish a unique flavour. Perhaps best of all, it comes together in minutes, making this a great quick-meal option. Serve it with some plain rice or pulao.

1 Put the prawns into a bowl with all the dry rub ingredients and rub them thoroughly over the prawns. Cover the bowl and leave to rest in the refrigerator for 15 minutes while you prepare the masala.

2 Heat the oil in a large saucepan over a medium heat. Add the curry leaves and the mustard and fennel seeds and let them sizzle for a few seconds. Now stir in the green chillies and onions and cook for 2–3 minutes, until they begin to soften.

Spinach and Coconut Dal

SERVES 4

FOR THE LENTILS
250 g (9 oz) toor dal
  (split pigeon peas)
1.2 litres (2 pints)
  water
1 ¼ teaspoons salt
1 teaspoons ground
  turmeric

FOR THE SPINACH
1 tablespoon ghee
1 tablespoon urad dal
  (whole black lentils)
1 teaspoon cumin
  seeds
2 teaspoons coriander
  seeds
½ teaspoon freshly
  ground black pepper
4 dried red chillies
50 g (1 ¾ oz) fresh
  coconut, roughly
  chopped
200 g (7 oz) fresh
  spinach
100 ml (3 ½ fl oz)
  boiling water

FOR THE TADKA
1 teaspoon ghee
1 teaspoon black
  mustard seeds
2 dried red chillies
a pinch of asafoetida

Spinach and lentils are a very typical combination and I have got a few ways to cook them together, but this particular recipe is special. It flavours the spinach with lovely spices and coconut, making the taste unique. You can eat a bowl of this on its own, or serve it with rice.

1 Start by combining the lentils, measured water, salt and turmeric in a pan and bringing them to the boil. Reduce the heat, then cover and cook for 40–45 minutes, until the lentils are soft.

2 To cook the spinach, heat the ghee in another pan and add the urad dal. Cook for 2 minutes over a low heat until slightly golden, then add the cumin seeds, coriander seeds, black pepper, dried red chillies and chopped coconut. Let it all sizzle for a minute.

3 Add the spinach and measured boiling water. Cover and cook over a low heat for 2 minutes, until the spinach has wilted. Transfer the mixture to a blender and blitz to a purée.

4 Tip the purée into the pan of cooked lentils and return to the boil.

5 For the tadka, heat the ghee in a small pan. Add the mustard seeds, dried red chillies and asafoetida and let them sizzle for a minute. Stir this mixture into the lentils and serve.

6 Store in an airtight container in the refrigerator for 2–3 days. Reheat well before serving.

Garlic and Tamarind Rasam

FOR THE RASAM
12–14 garlic cloves,
  thinly sliced
½ teaspoon salt
½ teaspoon ground
  turmeric
200 ml (7 fl oz) water
1 tablespoon ghee
1 teaspoon cumin
  seeds
2 dried red chillies
¼ teaspoon black
  peppercorns
1 tablespoon tamarind
  paste
800 ml (27 fl oz)
  boiling water

FOR THE TADKA
1 tablespoon ghee
1 teaspoon black
  mustard seeds
10 fresh curry leaves
1 tablespoon dark
  muscovado sugar
½ teaspoon salt

I didn't realize how many varieties of rasam there are in South Indian cooking until I visited my friend Renushree, who told me all about them as she made this incredible version. To begin with, I wasn't sure about the quantity of garlic – 12 to 14 cloves! – but it's one of the most amazing dishes I've eaten. The sour tamarind bounces off the sweetness of the sugar, and the garlic isn't overwhelming but melt-in-your-mouth sweet. This is perfect for when you're feeling run down.

1 Put the garlic, salt and turmeric into a pan with measured water and bring to the boil. Cook over a low heat for 20 minutes, until the garlic is soft.

2 In a small pan, heat the ghee. Add the cumin seeds, dried chillies and peppercorns and fry for a few seconds, until golden. Crush this mixture with a pestle and mortar, then add it to the pan of garlic.

3 Add the tamarind paste and the measured boiling water to the garlic too, then continue to cook over low heat for 10 minutes so that all the flavours can infuse.

4 To make the tadka, heat the ghee in a small pan. Add the mustard seeds and when they start to pop, remove the pan from the heat and add the curry leaves, muscovado sugar and salt.

5 Pour this over the rasam and serve immediately in small heatproof glasses or bowls to drink straight up.

6 This will keep in an airtight container in the refrigerator for 4–5 days. It is best to bring it to a boil before serving but do try it cold as well.

Black Lentils with Red Kidney Beans

SERVES 4–6

300 g (10½ oz) urad dal
(whole black lentils)
100 g (3½ oz) dried
red kidney beans
roughly 500 ml
(18 fl oz) water,
for soaking
1.4 litres (2½ pints)
water
1½ teaspoons salt
4 black cardamom
pods
1 tablespoon ghee
4 garlic cloves, finely
chopped
1 small green chilli,
finely chopped
2 tablespoons tomato
purée
1 tablespoon garam
masala
1 teaspoon chilli
powder
100–200 ml (3½
–7 fl oz) boiling
water, to loosen, if
required
1 tablespoon double
cream

TO GARNISH
1 tablespoon chopped
fresh coriander
1 small green chilli,
thinly sliced

My kids tell me this is one of their favourite lentil dishes. Cooking it with love, slowly over a low heat, brings out the flavour of the black lentils and black cardamom and results in a rich, intense, deep taste. And the best part is that it tastes even better the next day, so be sure to make a little extra. Serve it with rice, naan or chapatti.

1 Soak the lentils and beans in the measured soaking water for 4–5 hours.

2 Transfer the pulses and their soaking water to a deep saucepan and add the measured water, plus the salt and black cardamom pods. Bring the liquid to the boil, then cover the pan with a lid and simmer over a low heat for 1 hour or until the lentils and beans are cooked.

3 In a separate large saucepan, heat the ghee over a low heat, then add the garlic and chilli and cook for 1 minute. Stir in the tomato purée, garam masala and chilli powder and cook for another minute.

4 Tip the cooked lentils and beans into the pan of spices, mixing well. Cover the pan with a lid and cook over a low heat for 1–1½ hours, stirring every 10–15 minutes to ensure the mixture does not stick to the base of the pan. If the lentils become too thick during cooking, add just enough of the measured boiling water to loosen the mixture.

5 Finally, when the dal is ready, add the cream and mix well. Garnish with the coriander and sliced chilli and serve immediately with rice, naan or chapatti.

Five Lentils

SERVES 4

100 g (3½ oz) moong
  dal (split mung beans)
100 g (3½ oz) chana
  dal (split chickpeas)
100 g (3½ oz) moong
  sabut (whole green
  mung beans)
50 g (1¾ oz) urad dal
  (whole black lentils)
50 g (1¾ oz) toor dal
  (split pigeon peas)
500 ml (18 fl oz) cold
  water, for soaking
1 teaspoon salt
500 ml (18 fl oz)
  boiling water
1 tablespoon chopped
  fresh coriander, to
  garnish (optional)

FOR THE
TEMPERING

1 tablespoon ghee
pinch of asafoetida
2.5 cm (1 inch) piece
  of fresh root ginger,
  peeled and julienned
1 onion, thinly sliced
1 small green chilli,
  thinly sliced
1 tomato, thinly sliced
½ teaspoon chilli
  powder
½ teaspoon ground
  cumin
½ teaspoon amchur
  (mango powder)
½ teaspoon salt

Each lentil variety in this extraordinary dish brings its unique flavour, but feel free to skip one or two if you don't have them all to hand – simply increase the quantities of the others to fill the gap. The dish is deceptively simple to make. It is the tempering (adding fried spices, onion, chilli and other flavourings at the end of cooking) that gives it an impressive colour boost and flavour kick. Serve the dal with rice or chapatti.

1 Soak all the lentils together in the measured soaking water in a deep saucepan for 2–3 hours. When they have swollen, transfer the pan to the hob, stir in the salt and bring the mixture to the boil. Once boiling, half-cover the pan with a lid, reduce the heat to low and simmer for 30 minutes. Once the cooking time has elapsed, add the measured boiling water to the pan and continue to cook for 30 minutes or until the lentils are soft.

2 Heat the ghee in a saucepan over a medium heat. Add the asafoetida. After a minute or so, when it starts to sizzle and smells fragrant, mix in the ginger and cook for 1 minute. Next, stir in the onion and chilli and cook for 4–5 minutes, until the onion is soft.

3 Stir the tomato slices into the onion mixture and cook for 2 minutes, until they just begin to soften. Now add the chilli powder, cumin, amchur and salt, mix well and cook for 1 minute more.

4 Pour the lentils into a deep serving bowl and spoon the onion mixture over the top. Garnish with chopped coriander, if liked, and serve warm.

RICE
& BREADS

Cumin Rice

SERVES 4

1 tablespoon sunflower
oil

1 tablespoon ghee

2 teaspoons cumin
seeds

1½ teaspoons salt

300 g (10½ oz)
basmati rice, washed
and drained

1 teaspoon ground
cumin

1 teaspoon chilli
powder

20 g (¾ oz) fresh
coriander leaves,
finely chopped

700 ml (1¼ pints)
boiling water

As the name suggests, this dish has tons of cumin in it –
both whole and ground seeds – giving it a wonderful earthy,
comforting warmth. Try it as a simple rice accompaniment for
all the lovely curries in this book. To be honest, I'd happily
eat this rice with just some yogurt.

1 Heat the oil and ghee in a saucepan over a medium–low
   heat, then add the cumin seeds. Cook for a few seconds
   until they begin to sizzle. Stir in the salt, then add the rice
   and stir well. Next, add the spices and coriander, then
   the measured boiling water. Cover the pan with a lid and
   cook over a low heat for 15 minutes.

2 Once the cooking time has elapsed, turn off the heat but
   don't lift off the lid. Leave the rice to rest for 15 minutes
   before serving.

Peanut, Coriander and Lemon Rice

SERVES 4

2 tablespoons
groundnut oil
60 g (2¼ oz) blanched
peanuts
1 teaspoon mustard
seeds
12–14 fresh curry
leaves
1 onion, thinly sliced
2 green chillies, thinly
sliced
handful of fresh
coriander leaves,
roughly chopped
1 teaspoon salt
1 teaspoon chilli
powder
1 teaspoon ground
turmeric
1 teaspoon ground
cumin
300 g (10½ oz)
basmati rice, washed
and drained
grated zest and juice
of 2 lemons
600 ml (20 fl oz)
boiling water

This simple peanut-lemon rice with lots of coriander and curry leaves is seriously delicious. Because it is ready within minutes, it's perfect for when you need a substantial snack (have it with your favourite chutney), but it also makes a lovely accompaniment to any curry.

1 Heat the oil in a saucepan, then add the peanuts. Cook over a medium–low heat for 2 minutes until golden. Stir in the mustard seeds and curry leaves and let them sizzle for a few seconds, then mix in the onion and chillies. Cook for 5 minutes until they have softened.

2 Next, add the coriander, salt and spices to the pan and mix well. Now add the rice and stir until all the rice is coated well. Mix in the lemon zest and measured boiling water, cover the pan with a lid and cook over a low heat for 10 minutes until the rice is almost cooked.

3 Lift off the lid, pour in the lemon juice evenly across the top of the rice, then replace the lid and cook over a low heat for 5 minutes until the rice is fully cooked. Leave to rest without taking the lid off for about 10 minutes before serving.

Bengali Khichdi

130 g (4½ oz) moong
  dal (split mung beans)
130 g (4½ oz) basmati
  rice
500 ml (18 fl oz) water
1 tablespoon ghee
1 cinnamon stick
4 green cardamom
  pods
6 cloves
2 cm (¾ inch) fresh
  ginger, peeled and
  grated
1 teaspoon salt
½ teaspoon sugar
1 teaspoon ground
  turmeric
½ teaspoon chilli
  powder
2 tomatoes, roughly
  chopped
650 ml (22 fl oz)
  boiling water

FOR THE TADKA
1 tablespoon ghee
2 green chillies, thinly
  sliced
20 g (¾ oz) fresh
  coriander leaves,
  finely chopped

I enjoyed this stunning khichdi at the home of Ranjana, who runs a takeaway khichdi business in Delhi called Bhaat. It's a dish from her menu. I love that it's such a simple, one-pot meal – the sort of dish that's incredibly comforting to eat on a cold day – yet the flavours are truly amazing. All it needs is a side of raita.

1 Toast the moong dal in a dry pan over a low heat for 4–5 minutes, until it starts to change colour. Put it into a pan with the rice and rinse well, two or three times, with water. Drain, then soak the dal and rice in the measured water for an hour.

2 Heat the ghee in a large pan. Add the cinnamon, cardamom, cloves and ginger and cook for a minute over a low heat. Add the salt, sugar, turmeric and chilli powder and cook for a few seconds, then stir in the tomatoes.

3 Drain the dal and rice and add them to the pan. Cook, stirring, over a high heat for 2 minutes. Pour in the measured boiling water, then cover and cook over a low heat for 15 minutes, until the dal and rice are soft and squishy.

4 To make the tadka, melt the ghee in a small pan. Add the green chillies and let them sizzle for a few seconds, then add the coriander leaves. Pour the mixture over the khichdi and serve warm.

5 This can be stored in an airtight container in the refrigerator for 4–5 days. Heat thoroughly before serving.

Aubergine and Potato Rice

SERVES 4

FOR THE SPICE MIX

2 tablespoons urad dal (whole black lentils)
2 tablespoons coriander seeds
1 tablespoon chana dal (split chickpeas)
1 cinnamon stick
2 dried red chillies
6 cloves

FOR THE RICE

900 g (2 lb) cooked basmati rice or 300 g (10½ oz) uncooked rice
2 tablespoons sunflower oil
1 teaspoon black mustard seeds
2 red onions, thinly sliced
1 potato, halved lengthways and cut into 5 mm (¼ inch) slices
1 large aubergine, halved lengthways and cut into 5 mm (¼ inch) slices
1 teaspoon salt
½ teaspoon ground turmeric

When you've got leftover rice in the refrigerator, this makes a fabulous one-pot meal that simply needs a dollop of raita to serve. In fact, it's wonderful even without the rice! Feel free to eat the aubergine and potato mixture with chapatti or naan.

1 If you have not already done so, boil the rice according to the packet instructions and drain if necessary.

2 To make the spice mix, put all the ingredients into a dry pan and toast on a low heat for 2 minutes, until they change colour. Leave to cool slightly, then grind to a powder using a small blender or a spice grinder.

3 Heat the oil in a large pan over a medium heat. Add the mustard seeds and, when they begin to sizzle, add the onions and cook for 5–7 minutes, until they start to change colour. Mix in the potato, then cover and cook over a low heat for 5 minutes – the potato will start to soften but should not be cooked through yet.

4 Add the aubergine slices, stir well, then cover and cook over a low heat for 10 minutes, until the potato and aubergine are fully cooked. Add your spice powder, plus the salt and turmeric, and cook over a low heat for 1 minute.

5 Finally, add the cooked rice and turn the heat to high. Stir until the rice and vegetables are well mixed and hot through, then serve.

6 Store in an airtight container in the refrigerator for 4–5 days. Reheat before serving.

Vegetable Pulao

SERVES 4

1 tablespoon sunflower oil

1 onion, finely chopped

6 spring onions, finely chopped

1 green pepper, finely chopped

2 tomatoes, finely chopped

150g (5½ oz) fresh or frozen peas

1 teaspoon salt

1 teaspoon garam masala

½ teaspoon ground turmeric

¼ teaspoon freshly ground black pepper

4 servings of cooked basmati rice

Made right in front of you on the streets of Mumbai, this vegetarian pulao is super-delicious. In Mumbai they serve it with potato curry, green chutney and a little raita, which is a great combination, but you can also enjoy this satisfying rice dish on its own.

1 Heat the oil in a saucepan over a medium heat. Add the onion and cook for about 5 minutes, until softened. Reserve a handful of the green parts of the spring onion for garnish and add the rest to the onion in the pan. Cook for 2 minutes, until the spring onion begins to soften, then add the green pepper and tomatoes and mix well to combine.

2 If using frozen peas, blanch them in boiling water for 2 minutes and drain before use. Add the fresh or blanched frozen peas to the onion, mix well and cook for 2 minutes, until well combined, then stir in the salt, garam masala, turmeric and black pepper.

3 Stir the cooked rice into the saucepan and cook for a final 4–5 minutes, until the rice is heated through, then remove from the heat and serve hot, garnished with the reserved spring onion.

Quick Naan

MAKES 4

220 g (7¾ oz) self-
raising flour, plus
extra for dusting
¼ teaspoon salt
¼ teaspoon chilli
flakes
¼ teaspoon nigella
seeds
200 ml (7 fl oz) natural
yogurt
salted butter or ghee,
to serve

This is a super-simple and quick naan recipe. Adding baking powder and yogurt to the dough creates fluffy, pillowy naan breads that are ready in minutes. Once made, you can top the naan with garlic, chilli and coriander if you like.

1 Mix the flour, salt, chilli flakes and nigella seeds in a mixing bowl. Add the yogurt and mix well with your hands to form a dough. The dough may be slightly sticky at first, but continue to knead it for 2–3 minutes until it becomes a little smoother. Leave the dough in the bowl, cover the bowl with a clean tea towel and let the dough rest for 5 minutes.

2 Heat a frying pan or griddle pan over a medium heat. Divide the dough into 4 equal portions. Dust your work surface with a little flour, then roll out each dough portion into a circle with a diameter of 13–15 cm (5–6 inches). Cook in the hot pan for 1 minute on each side until golden.

3 Once cooked, brush each naan with butter or ghee and serve nice and hot.

Basic Chapatti

MAKES 12
300 g (10½ oz)
  chapatti flour, plus
  extra for dusting
roughly 175 ml
  (6 fl oz) water
ghee, to serve

There are many different recipes for making chapatti, but this is the way my family has made them for generations. Our version is a healthy one – there is no added salt, oil or any other ingredient, just flour and water, which gives you perfect, simple chapatti that taste amazing. Use them to scoop up sabjis, curries, chutneys and pickles, and as wraps.

1 Put the flour into a bowl. Very slowly, mix in just enough of the measured water to bring the mixture together in a dough – you might not need all the water or you may need a little more, so add just a few drops at a time. This is the best way to achieve a dough that is the correct consistency: smooth but not sticky.

2 Once the dough has come together, knead it on a clean surface for 2 minutes. Leave it to rest, either in a covered bowl or an airtight box, for 15–20 minutes.

3 Divide the dough into 12 equal portions. Roll each portion into a ball in your hands, then roll each ball in a little flour to dust. Using a rolling pin, roll out each ball into a circle with a diameter of 15–18 cm (6–7 inches).

4 Heat a skillet over a medium heat until hot. Carefully transfer one rolled-out portion of dough to the hot skillet and cook it for a few seconds on the first side, then turn. Allow the chapatti to bubble up a little on the second side, which will only take a few seconds, then turn it over again and cook for a few seconds, until it is golden and cooked through, pressing gently on the edges with some kitchen paper or a clean tea towel, which encourages the flatbread to puff up a little. Transfer the chapatti to a serving plate and spread a tiny amount of ghee across the top surface. Keep hot while you repeat the process with the remaining portions of dough. The best way to keep your chapatti soft and warm until serving is to wrap them in foil or in a clean tea towel until ready to eat. Serve the chapatti hot.

Parotha

300 g (10½ oz) plain
  flour, plus extra for
  dusting
1 teaspoon salt
2 teaspoons caster
  sugar
100 ml (3½ fl oz) milk
approximately 150 ml
  (¼ pint) sunflower
  oil
80 ml (2¾ fl oz) water

These flatbreads are inspired by the famous Malabar parothas of Kerala. The dough is straightforward enough to make, but you do need to give it time to rest between the various steps, and you can't be stingy with the oil! This way, the dough relaxes, allowing the lovely flaky layers to appear. Indeed, it's these dreamy layers that make this special flatbread perfect for your Sunday feasts.

1　Mix together the dry ingredients in a large bowl. Stir in the milk and 1 tablespoon oil. Add the measured water a little at a time and, using your hand, bring the mixture together to form a soft dough. Knead for 5 minutes, then place the dough in the bowl, cover the bowl with a clean tea towel and set aside to rest for 30 minutes.

2　Divide the dough into 4 equal portions and shape them into balls. Drizzle 1 teaspoon oil over each dough ball to cover. Cover with the tea towel and leave to rest for 30 minutes.

3　Working with 1 dough ball at a time, roll out the ball on a lightly oiled work surface into a thin circle, then drizzle over 1 teaspoon oil and spread it over the dough circle. Using your fingers, stretch the dough into a circle with a diameter of 30–35 cm (12–14 inches). Spread another teaspoon of oil over the circle, then pick up one side of the circle and fold it like a fan, pinching it together until you have a long, gathered piece of dough. Twist this around your thumb to make a spiral (like a cinnamon roll), then tuck the tail of the dough into the centre of the spiral. Cover with the tea towel and leave to rest for 30 minutes.

4 Again working on 1 piece at a time, roll out the twisted dough ball into a circle with a diameter of roughly 20 cm (8 inches).

5 Heat a frying pan to a high heat and, once hot, cook 1 parotha for 1 minute on each side. Now drizzle 1 teaspoon oil over the paratha and turn it over to cook that side again for 1 minute until golden. Meanwhile, drizzle 1 teaspoon oil over the surface now facing up. Once the underside is golden, flip the parotha and cook for another minute until both sides are golden. Transfer the cooked parotha to a clean surface and, using your hands, push the edges in towards the centre, encouraging the layers to open up. Repeat the process to cook the remaining parothas. Serve immediately.

Gram Flour Roti

MAKES 8

200 g (7 oz) chapatti
flour, plus extra for
dusting
50 g (1¾ oz) gram
flour (besan)
½ teaspoon salt
½ teaspoon ground
turmeric
½ teaspoon chilli
powder
2 tablespoons kasuri
methi (dried
fenugreek leaves)
1 tablespoon oil
120 ml (4 fl oz) water,
plus extra if needed
ghee

This is inspired by a traditional Gujarati flatbread called thepla, originally from western India but now popular all over the world – and with good reason! It's easy, versatile and delicious. My version makes it healthy as well. Serve it with anything you like, or just with some chutney.

1 Combine all the dry ingredients in a bowl. Mix in the oil, then gradually add just enough of the water (or a little more if necessary) to form a soft dough. Knead in the bowl for a couple of minutes or until smooth, then cover and leave to rest for 30 minutes.

2 Divide the dough into 8 equal portions. Taking one at a time, roll out on a lightly floured surface to a circle roughly 18 cm (7 inches) wide.

3 Heat a flat griddle or pan over a low–medium heat and, once hot, cook each roti for 1–2 minutes. Turn and cook for another minute on the other side, then remove to a plate. Brush a little ghee on top and serve warm.

4 The dough will keep in an airtight container in the refrigerator for 2–3 days.

Rava Dosa

MAKES 4

120 g (4¼ oz) semolina
120 g (4¼ oz) rice flour
60 g (2¼ oz) plain flour
1 teaspoon salt
½ teaspoon chilli powder
1 teaspoon cumin seeds
¼ teaspoon freshly ground black pepper
1 red onion, finely chopped
2.5 cm (1 inch) piece of fresh root ginger, peeled and finely chopped
10 fresh curry leaves, finely chopped
handful of fresh coriander leaves and stems, finely chopped
1 tablespoon natural yogurt
900 ml (1½ pints) water
sunflower oil, for cooking

This light and crispy type of dosa, made with rava (semolina), is quick to make compared with normal dosa, for which you need a few days for fermenting the rice and lentils. Rava dosas provide the perfect quick meal that still feels like a huge treat. Serve them with a bowl of dal or some coconut chutney for a feast with delicious South Indian flavours.

1   Put all the ingredients, except the water and oil, into a large bowl and mix well. Now add half the measured water and whisk until smooth. Add the remaining water and whisk again. Cover the bowl and set the mixture aside to rest for 30 minutes.

2   Heat a frying pan until it is smoking hot. Put a few drops of oil in the pan, then wipe them away with a sheet of kitchen paper so that the pan is clean. Now ladle in the batter in a large circle, adding just enough to create a thin layer with some holes in it. These are characteristic of rava dosa, so don't fill them up with more batter. Drizzle 1 teaspoon oil all around the edges of the dosa and cook over a medium heat for roughly 2 minutes until the dosa is golden and crispy. Fold in half and serve immediately. Continue cooking the rest of the dosa batter in the same way.

Masala Puri

MAKES 20
300 g (10½ oz) chapati
  flour, plus extra for
  dusting
½ teaspoon salt
½ teaspoon chilli
  powder
½ teaspoon ground
  turmeric
1 teaspoon ground
  coriander
1 teaspoon carom
  seeds (ajwain)
approximately 220–
  240 ml (7½–8½
  fl oz) water
sunflower oil, for
  deep-frying

Puri is a very popular type of bread in India and is often enjoyed at festivals, weddings and other special occasions. The dough is similar to chapati dough, but for this recipe I have added some lovely spices to it. The joy comes from deep-frying the dough until it puffs up. Puris are amazing served hot, but are often taken cold on picnics and train journeys in India to eat with some dry sabji (vegetable curry).

1 Put the flour, salt and spices into a bowl and mix well. Now slowly add just enough of the measured water (or more, if necessary) to bring the mixture together into a soft dough. Knead the dough for 2 minutes, then leave the dough in the bowl, cover the bowl with a clean tea towel and set aside to rest for 15–30 minutes.

2 Divide the dough into 20 equal portions and shape these into small balls. Working on a lightly floured surface, roll them out into thin circles with a diameter of roughly 7.5 cm (3 inches).

3 Heat enough oil for deep-frying in a deep, heavy-based saucepan or deep-fat fryer to 170–180°C (340–350°F). (Maintain this temperature range throughout cooking.) Gently place 1 puri into the oil and let it puff up. After 1 minute, turn it over in the oil and cook for another minute. Using a slotted spoon, remove the puri from the oil and transfer it to a bowl. Cook the remaining puris one at a time in this way. Serve immediately.

CHUTNEYS & SIDES

Mango Chutney

SERVES 6–8

2 tablespoons
sunflower oil

1 teaspoon nigella
seeds

4 garlic cloves, finely
chopped

1 cm (½ inch) piece
of fresh root ginger,
peeled and finely
chopped

3 red chillies, finely
chopped

½ teaspoon salt

¼ teaspoon ground
turmeric

¼ teaspoon ground
cinnamon

¼ teaspoon ground
cardamom

¼ teaspoon ground
cumin

¼ teaspoon ground
coriander

2 large mangoes,
peeled, stoned and
cut into 1–2 cm
(½–¾ inch) pieces

150 g (5½ oz) caster
sugar

3 tablespoons white
vinegar

There are so many snacks this chutney works well with, and it's also great in sandwiches, salads and much more. I'm not the biggest fan of sweet chutneys – I like them with a bit of spice and a kick of chilli – so while this chutney certainly ticks the sweet box, it is vibrant and alive.

1 Heat the oil in a saucepan over a medium–low heat, then add the nigella seeds. Cook for a few seconds until they begin to sizzle, then stir in the garlic, ginger and chillies and let them cook for a few seconds. Now add the salt and spices, followed by the mangoes, and mix well, then stir in the sugar. Next, add the vinegar and mix well, then cover the pan with a lid and cook over a low heat for 50–60 minutes, stirring occasionally, until the mangoes have softened and the chutney has thickened. Leave to cool completely before serving.

2 Store in an airtight container in the refrigerator for up to 2 weeks.

Garlic Pickle

40 garlic cloves, peeled

2 tablespoons mustard oil

10 small green chillies, quartered lengthways

1 teaspoon salt

1 teaspoon chilli powder

1 teaspoon ground turmeric

1 tablespoon grated or roughly chopped jaggery

FOR THE SPICE BLEND

2 teaspoons fenugreek seeds

2 teaspoons black mustard seeds

2 teaspoons cumin seeds

2 teaspoons coriander seeds

Almost any Indian dish can be paired with this delicious, strongly flavoured pickle, which has a pleasing smoky hint and a good chilli hit. Whether you serve it alongside lentils, chicken, fish or veg, it's bound to make the meal more special.

1 First, make the spice blend. Heat a dry frying pan over a low heat. Add the seeds and toast them for about 2 minutes, until they are fragrant and you can see them starting to smoke – but don't let them colour or burn! Use a pestle and mortar to grind the toasted seeds to a rough powder. Set aside.

2 Chop any really large garlic cloves lengthways into smaller pieces so that all the pieces of garlic are of a similar size.

3 Heat the oil in a saucepan over a low heat. When it is smoking hot, add the garlic and green chillies and cook for 5–7 minutes, until the garlic begins to soften but doesn't colour.

4 Add the spice blend along with the salt, chilli powder, turmeric and jaggery. Mix well and cook for 2 minutes, until the jaggery has melted.

5 Spoon the mixture into a sterilized jar and seal well. Leave the pickle to mature in a warm place for 1 week before serving. Once the jar is open, it will keep well in the refrigerator for up to 3 months.

Mango and Mint Chutney

MAKES ROUGHLY
200 G (7 OZ)

100 g (3½ oz) green
or unripe mango,
peeled and diced

40 g (1½ oz) mint,
leaves picked

40 g (1½ oz) fresh
coriander

½ teaspoon salt

½ teaspoon sugar

2 small green chillies

1 tablespoon lime juice

4 tablespoons water

I love a good, herby, fresh green chutney and this one goes with almost any meal you might cook from this book. Using green mango adds a tangy flavour and a lovely summery note. If you can't find any small green mangoes, go for a big, really hard, unripe mango from the supermarket, which will work just as well.

1 Put all the ingredients into the bowl of a mini food processor. Whizz until smooth. Serve immediately.

2 This chutney will keep in an airtight container in the refrigerator for 4–5 days.

Carrot and Onion Pickle

MAKES ROUGHLY
600 G (1 LB 5 OZ)

2 carrots, cut into
  strips
2 red onions, thinly
  sliced
12 small green chillies,
  thinly sliced
2 pieces of fresh
  turmeric, peeled and
  thinly sliced
1 teaspoon salt
½ teaspoon chilli
  powder
2 teaspoons black
  mustard seeds,
  lightly crushed
150 ml (¼ pint) cider
  vinegar

You'll love this crunchy, fresh and spicy pickle. Serve it with any of the dishes in this book, but it's especially good with rice and lentils.

1 Mix all the ingredients together in a large bowl, ensuring they are well combined.

2 Pack the mixture into a sterilized jar and leave in a dark place for 24 hours. Transfer the jar to the refrigerator after that, where it will keep for 7–10 days.

Spinach Raita

SERVES 4

FOR THE RAITA
1 teaspoon sunflower oil
1 teaspoon cumin seeds
200 g (7 oz) fresh spinach leaves, finely chopped
200 g (7 oz) natural yogurt
¼ teaspoon salt
¼ teaspoon ground cumin

FOR THE TADKA
1 teaspoon sunflower oil
1 teaspoon black mustard seeds
1 garlic clove, finely chopped
2 dried red chillies
10 fresh curry leaves

I would be happy with just a bowl of this on its own – the garlic, curry leaves and chilli in the tadka taste amazing when added to the spinach yogurt. I tried this for the first time at my friend, Pranoti's house. She makes it often to serve with meals. You'll find it's great with any curry, in a wrap, with rice or bread – a real all-rounder.

1 To start the raita, heat the oil in a pan and add the cumin seeds. Once they start to sizzle, add the spinach leaves and cook, stirring, for 2 minutes on a high heat until the leaves have wilted and softened. Remove from the heat and leave to cool slightly.

2 In a bowl, combine the yogurt, salt and ground cumin, and stir in the wilted spiced spinach.

3 To make the tadka, heat the oil in a small pan and add the mustard seeds. Once they start to sizzle, add the garlic, dried red chillies and curry leaves and cook for a few seconds. Pour this into the raita, mix and serve.

Coriander and Mint Chutney

100 g (3½ oz) fresh
  coriander
100 g (3½ oz) fresh
  mint leaves
2 green chillies
juice of 1 lime
1 teaspoon salt
½ teaspoon sugar
3 tablespoons water

I've shared a coriander chutney in every book I've written, but it really is amazing and key to my kitchen: I have a jar of it in my refrigerator at all times and it will last three or four days. You can also freeze this in small portions, and simply take out to defrost as and when needed.

1 Put all the ingredients into a blender, grind to a smooth paste and serve.

Tamarind and Date Chutney

MAKES A SMALL
BOWL

50 g (1¾ oz) tamarind
pulp

50 g (1¾ oz) pitted
dates

50 g (1¾ oz) jaggery

350 ml (12 fl oz) water

½ teaspoon salt

1 teaspoon ground
cumin

1 teaspoon chilli
powder

1 teaspoon ground
ginger

1 teaspoon toasted
fennel seeds, lightly
crushed

Another of the chutneys I really can't do without! I make a big jar of this and keep it in the refrigerator to use over the course of six weeks or so. It's great when served with canapés, snacks, at barbecues and much more – a classic that will never go out of fashion.

1 Combine the tamarind, dates, jaggery and measured water in a pan. Bring to the boil, then reduce the heat to low and cook for 15–20 minutes.

2 Strain the mixture through a fine sieve into a jug, making sure you press down well on the ingredients to extract maximum flavour.

3 Return the sieved mixture in the jug to the pan and add the salt, cumin, chilli powder, ginger and fennel seeds. Cook gently for 2 minutes, then leave to cool before storing it in a jar.

SWEET THINGS

Almond Halwa

SERVES 4
100 g (3½ oz) unsalted butter or ghee
140 g (5 oz) ground almonds
140 ml (4¾ fl oz) milk
¼ teaspoon ground cardamom
pinch of saffron threads
40 g (1½ oz) golden caster sugar
handful of pistachio nuts, crushed

Halwa is one of the easiest Indian desserts to cook, and the ingredients are versatile – you can use nuts, semolina, lentils or flour. The almond version is usually made by soaking the whole nuts overnight, then peeling them, drying them and grinding them to a powder. I make the process quicker and easier by using ready-ground almonds – much less work for all the taste! Use ghee to cook this dish if you can – the flavours and oils released are delicious.

1 Heat the butter or ghee in a saucepan over a medium heat. Once it begins to bubble and sizzle, add the ground almonds and reduce the heat to low. Cook for 12–14 minutes, stirring every 2 minutes, until the mixture turns a deep golden colour.

2 Meanwhile, pour the milk into a jug, add the cardamom and saffron and stir well to combine. Set aside.

3 Add the sugar to the almond mixture in the pan and mix well. Continue to cook over a low heat for 2 minutes, stirring continuously to encourage the sugar to dissolve. Once the sugar has dissolved, slowly pour in the spiced milk, stirring continuously until the milk is incorporated. Now cook for 3–4 minutes until the mixture thickens. Take the pan off the heat, then sprinkle the crushed pistachios on top. Serve warm.

Walnut and Hazelnut Laddoos

MAKES 15
85 g (3 oz) walnuts
85 g (3 oz) hazelnuts
150 g (5 ½ oz) chapatti
   flour
3 tablespoons ghee
3 tablespoons agave
   nectar
1 teaspoon ground
   cardamom
¼ teaspoon rose water
dried rose petals,
   to decorate

Nuts add such a lovely flavour to these laddoos, and also help to bind them so they hold their shape well. Quick and simple to make, these tempting treats are scented with cardamom and also rose water, which adds a delicate, heart-warming floral touch. Laddoos are a great sweet with which to end a meal, but I warn you – it is difficult to stop at just one.

1 Put the nuts into a dry frying pan over a medium–low heat and toast them, stirring continuously, for 5 minutes or until they change colour.

2 Tip the toasted nuts into a mini food processor and blitz to a paste – keep blending until the nuts release their oil. Transfer the nut paste to a bowl.

3 Put the flour into the same dry frying pan and toast it over a low heat for 8–10 minutes, stirring continuously, until the flour is light golden and fragrant. Add the ghee and mix well – the mixture will start to look crumbly.

4 Add the flour mixture to the nut paste along with the agave nectar, cardamom and rose water. Use your hands to combine the mixture well.

5 Take a lime-sized portion of the laddoo mixture in the palm of your hand and compress it into a small ball. Set the laddoo on a serving dish and repeat the shaping process with the remaining mixture.

6 You can serve the laddoos immediately, decorated with dried rose petals, or store them in an airtight container in the refrigerator for 5–6 days. Bring them to room temperature before serving.

Vermicelli Rice Pudding

SERVES 2

500 ml (18 fl oz) whole milk

2 tablespoons ghee

30 g (1 oz) cashew nuts, roughly chopped

30 g (1 oz) blanched almonds, roughly chopped

30 g (1 oz) raisins – you can use a mixture of different raisins such as black, golden and green or just one type

40 g (1½ oz) roasted vermicelli

40 g (1½ oz) light soft brown sugar

pinch of ground cardamom

When I was little, my grandmother used to make the dough for vermicelli and then spend hours rolling the thin noodles by hand. The noodles would then be left on big steel plates in the sun for days to dry out. My mother has now taken up making vermicelli at home and the last time she came to visit she brought me a big bagful. Vermicelli is now widely available and these days you can buy it ready-roasted, cutting another 5 minutes off your cooking time.

1 Bring the milk to the boil in a pan, then take off the heat and set aside.

2 Heat the ghee in another pan, add the nuts and raisins and cook over a low heat for a minute until they start to change colour.

3 Add the vermicelli and stir well. Then gradually pour in the boiled milk and cook over a low heat for 10 minutes until the vermicelli is just soft.

4 Sprinkle in the sugar and cook for another 5 minutes until the milk is creamy and the vermicelli is cooked through. Then add the cardamom and mix well. Serve warm or at room temperature.

Cardamom and Pistachio Kulfi

SERVES 6

1.5 litres (2¾ pints) milk

50 g (1¾ oz) golden caster sugar

½ teaspoon ground cardamom

3 tablespoons finely chopped pistachio nuts, plus extra to decorate

Kulfi (Indian ice cream) is particularly popular in Delhi, where you find an astonishing variety of flavours these days, from chocolate and mint to paan, yet the traditional combination of cardamom and pistachios remains my favourite. Making kulfi requires patience – no short cuts can give the same amount of flavour as hours spent reducing the milk, so it's definitely worth the effort.

1 Pour the milk into a large, heavy-based saucepan. Bring it to the boil, then reduce the heat to low and simmer for 3 hours, stirring every 5–7 minutes to ensure the milk does not stick to the bottom of the pan.

2 Once the milk has reduced by two-thirds, measure it to ensure the volume has reduced to 500 ml (18 fl oz), then return it to the pan. Add the sugar and cardamom and stir for 1 minute, then add the pistachios. Pour the mixture into a jug and leave it to cool a little.

3 Divide the mixture between 6 kulfi cones (use plastic containers if you don't have any) and freeze overnight.

4 When ready to serve, dip the cones in warm water for a few seconds, then turn out the kulfi onto individual serving plates. Sprinkle with the extra pistachios to serve.

Carrot Halwa

SERVES 6
2 tablespoons ghee
500 g (1 lb 2 oz)
  carrots, peeled and
  grated
500 ml (18 fl oz) milk
50 g (1 ¾ oz)
  granulated sugar
½ teaspoon ground
  cardamom
25 g (1 oz) cashew
  nuts, roughly
  chopped
25 g (1 oz) almonds,
  roughly chopped,
  plus extra to
  decorate
raisins, to decorate

People make this sweet, comforting pudding, known as gajar ka halwa, in winter, when carrots come into season. You'll find it in Delhi and throughout Northern India. People prepare it at home or buy it from street stalls, where the vendors keep the dish warm on large skillets. It is often made with khoya, a thickened milk, but below is a recipe for a slightly lighter version, made with regular milk.

1 Heat the ghee in a wide saucepan over a medium heat. Add the grated carrot and cook for 5 minutes, until it changes colour. Add the milk and bring to a boil. Once the mixture is bubbling, reduce the heat to very low and cook for 40–45 minutes, uncovered, stirring every 5 minutes, until all the milk is absorbed by the carrot.

2 Add the sugar and cardamom to the pan and cook for 5 minutes, until the sugar has melted. Stir in the cashews and almonds. Serve either hot or cold, with the extra almonds and raisins sprinkled on top.

Saffron Barfi

MAKES 12
800 ml (27 fl oz) whole
  milk
a pinch of saffron
ghee, for greasing
60 g (2¼ oz)
  granulated sugar
¼ teaspoon ground
  cardamom
150 g (5½ oz) ground
  almonds
a handful of pistachio
  nuts, finely chopped

Barfis can be too sweet but not this delicately flavoured one, which has almonds, bringing an extra dimension of creaminess. It's easy to make but you do need patience, which is well rewarded with a gorgeous pudding.

1 Bring the milk slowly to simmering point in a pan. Add the saffron, reduce the heat to low and cook for 15 minutes, stirring every 2 minutes to prevent sticking.

2 Meanwhile, use some ghee and baking parchment to grease and line a 20 cm (8 inches) square loose-bottomed cake tin.

3 Once the 15 minutes is up, stir the sugar into the milk and cook for 10 minutes, still stirring every 2 minutes. Add the cardamom and almonds and mix well.

4 This is where you need to be patient: continue cooking for 20–25 minutes, stirring slowly the whole time. The mixture will gradually begin to thicken and come together, and will leave the sides of the pan.

5 Quickly tip the mixture into the prepared tin and spread out with a palette knife or the back of a spoon. Sprinkle the pistachios over the barfi and press them in. Leave to set completely. Cut into pieces to serve.

6 You can store this in the refrigerator for 3–4 days – just make sure to leave it at room temperature for about an hour before serving.

Fruit Chaat

SERVES 4
1 banana, peeled and
  roughly chopped
1 apple, cored and
  roughly chopped
seeds from ½
  pomegranate
½ yellow-fleshed
  cantaloupe melon,
  peeled, deseeded and
  roughly chopped
couple of watermelon
  slices, peeled,
  deseeded and
  roughly chopped
1 orange, peeled,
  deseeded and
  roughly chopped
½ teaspoon kala
  namak (black salt)
½ teaspoon chaat
  masala
¼ teaspoon chilli
  flakes
pinch of salt
pinch of freshly
  ground black pepper
2 tablespoons lemon
  juice

Spice up a simple bowl of fruit to make it even more refreshing. The sour, zingy spices work beautifully with the sweet, crisp freshness of the fruit. Fruit chaat is a popular Indian street food, and vendors often vary the spice blend to suit the combination of fruits. I'm a big fan of this particular combo.

1 Put all the prepared fruits into a bowl, add the spices, salt and pepper and lemon juice, then mix well. Serve immediately.

Nimbu Paani

SERVES 4

125 ml (4 fl oz) lemon
  juice
juice of 2 limes
4 tablespoons icing
  sugar
½ teaspoon salt
½–¾ teaspoon kala
  namak (black salt)
8 drops of rose water
800 ml (27 fl oz)
  cold water
ice cubes, to serve

Like a rose-scented lemonade, this is one of those refreshing drinks found on every corner of every street in India during the summer. The black salt adds a lovely spicy sourness to the taste of the citrus fruits.

1 Combine the citrus juices in a jug. Add the icing sugar, salts and rose water and mix until the sugar has dissolved. Stir in the measured water.

2 Put some ice into 4 glasses, pour over the nimbu paani and serve.

Mango Lassi

SERVES 3

seeds from 5 green
  cardamom pods
200 g (7 oz) mango
  pulp
200 ml (7 fl oz)
  natural yogurt
100 ml (3½ fl oz) milk
1 tablespoon
  granulated sugar
ice cubes, to serve

I first had this delicious mango lassi in Delhi and, since then, have always made it at home during mango season. In India, lassi is considered a hot summer's drink as the ice and yogurt help you to cool down.

1 Using a pestle and mortar, grind the cardamom seeds to a powder.

2 Combine the mango pulp, yogurt, milk, sugar and ground cardamom in a blender. Add the ice cubes and blitz for 1 minute. Pour into 3 glasses and serve immediately.

Masala Chai

300 ml (½ pint) water
1 thick slice of fresh
  root ginger, peeled
  and squashed
2 green cardamom
  pods
2 cloves
2 teaspoons
  granulated sugar
1 tablespoon loose-
  leaf tea or 2 tea bags
5 tablespoons milk

The backbone of Indian street food culture, this drink is available in every nook and cranny of almost every street in India. Everyone has their favourite chai stalls, which they'll visit daily, whether it's day or night. When I was in my final year of college and we were working late at night, a chai walla would come to the gate on a bicycle at around 1am with piping hot chai in a container. All the students who were still up would go and sit in a big group just outside the college to take a break and drink tea together. I learned this masala chai recipe years ago from a tea stall holder in Delhi.

1 Combine the measured water, ginger, cardamom pods and cloves in a saucepan and bring to a boil. Add the sugar and tea, reduce the heat to low and cook for 2 minutes, until the mixture darkens to a deep, strong colour.

2 Stir the milk into the pan and return the mixture to a boil, then reduce the heat and simmer for 2–4 minutes, until well infused.

3 Pass the masala chai carefully through a sieve into 2 cups and serve immediately.

INDEX

GLOSSARY OF TERMS

UK	US
aubergine	eggplant
baking tray	baking sheet
barbecue	grill
beetroot	beets
cake tin	cake pan
caster sugar	superfine sugar
chickpeas	garbanzo beans
chilli/chillies	chili/chiles
chilli flakes	red pepper flakes
clingfilm	plastic wrap
coriander (fresh)	cilantro
cornflour	cornstarch
courgette	zucchini
desiccated coconut	unsweetened desiccated coconut
double cream	heavy cream
frying pan	skillet
gram flour	besan/chickpea flour
green pepper	green bell pepper
grill	broil/broiler
groundnut oil	peanut oil
hob	stove
icing sugar	confectioners' sugar
jug	pitcher
kitchen paper	paper towels
plain flour	all-purpose flour
rapeseed oil	canola oil
self-raising flour	self-rising flour
shops	stores
sieve	strainer
spring onions	scallions
Swiss roll	jelly roll
tea towel	dishtowel
tomato purée	tomato paste